NELSON and BATH

NELSON and BATH

Louis Hodgkin

THE NELSON SOCIETY

© Louis Hodgkin 2004

Published by The Nelson Society

First published 1991

Revised and enlarged edition 2004

ISBN 0-9537200-3-9

Available from The Publications Manager
The Nelson Society
16 Silver Lane, Billinghurst, West Sussex RH14 9RJ
Tel/Fax: 01403 782496

Design and Layout: Eddie Hams. Tel/Fax: 01425 476509

Printed by Pardy & Son (Printers), Parkside, Ringwood, Hampshire, BH24 3SF

CONTENTS

LIST OF ILLUSTRATIONS

INTRODUCTION

The format of this book is to give the reader a chance to find out more about the City of Bath through its associations with Nelson. His father came for his annual 'recruit' (recuperation), Nelson came for the cure, his wife lived in Bath for three years, and other members of his family came to visit and live for periods of time. Of Nelson's well trodden biography, this covers the period in which he established himself, the first 25 years of his life at sea, married Frances Nisbet, lost the sight in his famous 'blind' eye, lost his arm, and rose to the rank of Rear Admiral. Leaving Bath for the last time, his fame grew with his dramatic victories at the Nile, Copenhagen, Trafalgar, and his passionate public affair with Emma, Lady Hamilton. Naval connections did not stop there, and continue today with the management of the HMS *Victory*, by the Ministry of Defence based in the City.

The links with the City are legion and it would be foolish to suggest that this account is anywhere complete. Hopefully, the main points have been covered that relate to Nelson and his wife. The aim is to offer a breadth to the subject. The majority of sources used are the published correspondence of Nelson in *Dispatches and Letters of Admiral Lord Nelson* by Nicolas, and *Nelson's Letters to His Wife and other documents 1785-1831*, edited by G.P. Naish. The latter were drawn mainly from the collection of letters held at the Monmouth Museum in Gwent made by Lady Llangattock, as well as the National Maritime Museum, Greenwich.

Over the years I have had great support from members of The Nelson Society, as an organisation the Western Group, and in particular the late Phil Knight who enthused about the amount of information available. Most of all I must thank Bronwyn Williams-Ellis who for years has patiently listened to the information as it percolated through and been a great support.

Louis Hodgkin

Silhouette of the Reverend Edmund Nelson as he appeared on his many visits to Bath to recover his health. After M. Eyre Matcham, *The Nelson of Burnham Thorpe*, 1911.

EDMUND NELSON AND HIS FAMILY IN BATH

The Reverend Edmund Nelson was Rector of the small Norfolk parish of Burham Thorpe, married to Catherine, née Suckling, and where Horatio Nelson was born. Unfortunately Catherine was to die when Nelson was only nine years old, leaving the country parson with seven children, four sons and three daughters. It is after the death of his wife that he would take his annual 'recruit' (recuperation), for his health, always a concern, a combination of rheumatics and weak chest, which would entail an annual visit to Bath for the 'cure'.

Nelson's uncle, Maurice Suckling, a Captain in the Royal Navy, succeeded, whilst in the West Indies, in defeating a small French squadron in 1759, an event always celebrated in the Nelson household on 21 October. Hostilities in the Falkland Islands inspired the young Horatio to ask whether he could join his uncle preparing his new ship *Raisonnable* at Chatham. Horatio persuaded his brother William to write to their father in Bath in January 1771, to get his father's permission. The Rector was only too pleased to agree; by contrast Captain Suckling was to exclaim: ' What has poor Horace done, who is so weak that he above all the rest should rough it out at sea? But let him come; and the first time we go into action, a cannon ball may knock off his head, and provide for him at once'.

So, in January 1771, Horatio Nelson was entered into the books of the *Raisonnable* to begin his naval career at the age of twelve.

Later, as the Reverend Nelson's daughters grew older, what better place than Bath was there to find positions for the two youngest daughters, Susannah and Kitty (sometimes known as Catherine), both of whom worked as milliners in Messrs Walters, Milsom Street, Bath. Family friends, the Scriveners from Norfolk, who now lived in Bath would keep an eye on the two young women when Edmund had returned to his parish.

At the death of their uncle Maurice Suckling in 1778 who, although married had died without issue, left all the Nelson children a legacy: the four sons received £500 each and the three daughters £1000 each. For the daughters, it gave them enough independence for them to give up their occupations. The eldest, Ann, who had been indentured to a lace manufactory on Ludgate Hill, London, on receipt of her legacy came to live in Bath in New King Street. There is an unconfirmed story that Ann had a son by the manager of the factory, a Mr Robinson; she left the son with the father when she went to Bath. After much investigation there is no evidence to confirm this. Disaster struck when Ann caught a chill after attending the New Assembly Rooms in Bath, dying two weeks later aged 23 years, at her lodgings in New King Street (reported in the *Bath Chronicle*, 15 November 1783) . She is buried in a sarcophagus under a yew tree in Bathford Churchyard, where her

Ann Nelson's grave, died April 1783, in Bathford Churchyard, where her father occasionally officiated. Alongside are the graves of Elizabeth Matcham and William Matcham, the mother-in-law and son of Catherine Matcham, nèe Nelson, both sisters to Nelson. An old postcard shows the graves with railings, which no longer exist.

father officiated as parish priest in the place of the incumbent, the Reverend John Berjeu.

Susannah had been apprenticed for three years, and had married a corn merchant, Thomas Bolton, from Wells-next-the-Sea, in Norfolk. After a brief spell in the Low Countries, they settled down to farm in Cranwitch, Suffolk. It is through her descent that the title of Earl Nelson has passed to the present day.

Catherine, or Kitty, the youngest, after four 'seasons' in Bath met and married George Matcham, an explorer, who had inherited an East Indian fortune. Later resident in Bath with their large family, they cared for their father Edmund Nelson through his final days in Pultney Street, Bath, in April 1802. He was later buried in Burnham Thorpe.

POST CAPTAIN, SICK AND EXHAUSTED, NELSON'S FIRST VISIT TO BATH AND TREATMENT 1781

Ten years after he had asked his father's permission to go to sea, Horatio Nelson arrived at Bath in January 1781, an invalid barely able to walk, to his hastily arranged lodgings in the home of the apothecary Joseph Spry at 2 Pierrepont Street.

Nelson had risen to the rank of Post Captain. His sea service was considerable, having been into the Arctic, to the East Indies, America and the West Indies. The cause of his fever was an expedition up the San Juan river in Nicaragua in a vain attempt to cut the Spanish Colonies North and South in Central America. Badly planned, there was little hope of success, with 80% of the ship's crew of the *Hichinbrooke* sick in the first 24 hours. Capturing the San Juan Castle (El Castillo de la Imaculada da Conception, or, to the British, St John's Castle) that guarded the river and, unable to hold it, Nelson had to retreat due his health, and forgo his new command and return home.

Edmund Nelson, his father, lodged over the road in 9 Pierrepont Street, and nursed his son on arrival until he became more mobile. Nelson occupied the front room on the ground floor at no. 2, at ten shillings (50p) a week. The only accounts of Nelson's time in Bath are letters to his 'sea daddy', Captain William Locker, with whom he had served as a young Lieutenant in the *Lowestoffe*. He wrote: ' I have been so ill since I have been here, that I was obliged to be carried to and fro from bed, with the most excruciating tortures, but thank God, I am now upon the mending hand. I am physicked three times a day, drink the waters and bathe every other night, besides not drinking wine, which I think the worst of all'. Throughout, the Rector was at his son's side.

Bathing could take place in four baths, the King or Queen Baths, the Hot Bath

One of the few buildings remaining that Nelson would recognise from his stay in Bath for the cure in 1781 is 2 Pierrepont Street. Many of the buildings associated with the hero have been pulled down, not least his birthplace, the Rectory at Burnham Thorpe.

The Pump Room where the waters were taken by both Nelson and his father. Prescriptions could range from a glass to three gallons a day. In 1784 Nelson came to visit his father in Bath who was very frail but, no doubt helped by his annual 'recruit', the waters helped him to survive until 1802. The Greek inscription on the pediment, 'Ariston men hydor', translates as 'Water is best', and is the first line of Pindar's first Olympic Ode.

or the Cross Bath, but which one Nelson used is not known. I have chosen as an example, the Cross Bath at the end of Bath Street. It is an elegant building which now forms part of the new Thermae Bath Spa.

The Cross Bath, dating from the 14th century, is named after the monument erected by Lord Melfont who was Secretary of State to James II, following the successful visit of Mary of Modena in 1687. The bath is small, measuring roughly 24ft by 19ft (7.3 x 5.7m), and even smaller when it included the 'cross' in the middle, removed in 1783. Originally the water fed directly from the springs of thermal water at a temperature of 30 degrees centigrade. The building today is the result of improvements started by Thomas Baldwin and completed by John Palmer in 1784; they had been impressed on the City by local doctors due to the unsanitary conditions. The bath remained in use by the Royal Mineral Hospital for rheumatic diseases until the 1970s. As part of the 'Spa' Millennium project the bath has undergone another revamp by the architect Nicholas Grimshaw, who restored the pool to its original oval shape and it now forms part of the Thermae Bath Spa.

The cost of bathing was not cheap in the 1780s, 1s 6d (7½p) for admission that included a towel and a bathing costume. For men this consisted of shorts and a waistcoat, while for women there was what was described as a 'parson's' gown which billowed with air as they descended into the water. The garments were made of linen which in time became yellow from the sulphur in the water. Bathing consisted of sitting up to the neck in the water, with an option to douse the ailing part of the body from the pump for 3d (1½p) a hundred strokes.

Prior to the improvements of 1784 a Dr Sutherland gives a description of the Cross Bath. 'The day began with bathing at an early hour sometimes under doctor's orders or more often as a diversion. There were five baths in all but only two were fashionable and frequented by the *beau monde*, the King's Bath and the Cross Bath. The corporation had not spent much on arranging or decorating them and so they were open to the sky, badly kept and surrounded by buildings; they were approached by narrow passages, niches in the walls afforded the only shelter obtainable from the wind and rain'. Dr Sutherland continues, ' the avenue which leads to the slips are dark and narrow, passages conspicuous than any inn. The slips resemble rather cells for the dead than dressing rooms for the living. Their walls and floors are composed of the same materials, cold stone, and eternally sweating with steam of the baths, dark as dungeons, and in their present condition incapable of being warmed. From the dressing room we descend by narrow steps into the unseemly ponds'. To counter this, nosegays and snuff boxes with handkerchiefs were floated in shallow wooden bowls for the bathers' convenience. Women would bathe around the edge of the pool while the men occupied the middle. A 'Sergeant' was on duty in one of the galleries to make sure of no improprieties, which could lead to a fine. In the other gallery would be a band to serenade the bathers. Tokens of gratitude for the cure took the form of copper rings with inscriptions mounted around the pool; the Cross Bath had 40 of these rings. Nelson mentions in his letter to Locker that to avoid the rush he bathed every other evening when most of the bathers had moved on to other attractions in the City.

Nelson's doctor, Dr Francis Woodward (1721-85), at 8 Gay Street, was a Cambridge graduate whose practice was described as 'being wide but not particularly profitable', and little is known of the man beyond his connection with Nelson. Nelson, writing to Locker, reported: 'I do not set under the hands of a Doctor very easily, although I give myself credit this once for having done everything, and taking every medicine that was ordered, that Dr Woodward who is my physician, said he had never had a better patient'. Medication consisted of a cordial and a bolus (a large pill). When it came to settling his bill Nelson queried the

Portrait of Dr Woodward by Thomas Beach that hangs in the Guildhall, Bath. When Nelson questioned his bill from the Doctor in 1781, he countered with: 'Pray Captain Nelson, allow me to follow what I consider to be my professional duty. Your illness Sir was brought on by serving your King and country, and believe me, I love both too well to be able to receive any more'. Photograph, Victoria Art Gallery, Bath.

amount; 'pray Captain Nelson', said the Doctor, 'allow me to follow what I consider my professional duty. Your illness Sir was brought on by serving your King and Country, and believe me, I love both too well to receive more'. Dr Woodward is buried in Walcot Churchyard, Bath.

At the Nelson Medical Symposium 2000, published by the Royal Naval Medical Service, Dr Ann-Mary Hills reassessed Nelson's ailments suggesting that in fact he suffered from Tropical Sprue whose symptoms are diahorrea, fever, malaise, and weakness. The result, no doubt, of poor rations and possibly contaminated water ashore in Nicaragua.

Gradually mid way through his stay in Bath he wrote to Locker: 'My health thank God is very near perfectly restored and I have the perfect use of all my limbs, except my left arm, which I can hardly tell what is the matter with it. From the

Portrait of Nelson by François Rigaud. The painting was commissioned in 1777 when Nelson was a Lieutenant in *Lowestoffe*, by the time he collected it, in 1781, after recovering his health in Bath, he had reached the rank of Post Captain, and his exploits on the 'Spanish Maine' were the talk of the town in Bath. National Maritime Museum, Greenwich.

shoulder to my fingers end are as if half dead; but surgeons and doctors give me hopes it will go off '.

As he recovered his health so Nelson was able to go about town and encounter various acquaintances. 'Bath was just like Jamaica, the hectic social activity, card playing and balls, the gouty old men eyeing the pretty young women amongst the rich planters on leave from the West Indies'. Nelson encountered Hercules Ross who had provisioned the expedition to Nicaragua, and Admiral Bickerton a well respected seaman whom Nelson had encountered in the West Indies and whose son was to serve Nelson later in the Mediterranean.

At the end of March 1781 Nelson left Bath for London, on half pay, to collect the first three-quarter length portrait, just completed by François Rigaud but started in 1778 when Nelson was only a Lieutenant. Altered to show his promotion to Post Captain, and to include the Fort on the San Juan River, it was given to Captain William Locker. Locker encouraged the commission, and later became Governor of Greenwich Hospital; the portrait can now be seen in the National Maritime Museum, Greenwich. Nelson resumed his command in August in the *Albermarle* for service initially in the Baltic and later on the American Station.

NELSON'S SEARCH FOR A WIFE AND FURTHER VISITS TO BATH 1784, 1788

Having rapidly gained promotion on the West Indies Station, Nelson's next ambition was to find a suitable wife. Spending long periods at sea did not offer many opportunities to meet women. Nelson's first attempt almost lead to a premature end to his naval career when he jumped ship whilst in Montreal in 1782 in pursuit of a certain Miss Mary Simpson who, it transpired, was more interested in army officers, acknowledged as wealthy having often purchased their commissions. A verse in her praise appeared in the *Quebec Gazette*:

> Sure you will listen to my call,
> Since beauty and Quebec's fair nymphs I sing.
> Henceforth Diana is Miss S-ps-n see,
> As noble and majestic her air…

A second attempt came during the brief Peace of Amiens in 1783. Nelson travelled to France and visited St Omer, and again fell 'in love' with a young English girl. About 20 years old, enchanted by her entertaining and singing, she was the daughter of an English clergyman with a large family. Miss Elizabeth Andrews rebuffed his advances, but offered sympathy to Nelson on hearing the news of the death of his sister Ann who had caught a chill on leaving the Assembly Rooms in Bath.

George Andrews, her brother, was to serve with distinction later as a midshipman alongside Nelson in the *Boreas* in 1786. He survived a duel, was reported as mortally wounded, rose to First Lieutenant in the *Agamemnon* (Nelson's 'favourite') from where he was promoted to Captain in 1796, he died a Post Captain in 1810. Miss Andrews married a clergyman named Farror and later, as her second husband, Colonel Roger Warne of the East India Service. Mrs Warne was to spend her last years in St James Square, Bath.

In January 1784 Nelson visited Bath to see his ailing father, staying again in 2 Pierrepont Street. He wrote to his brother William that he was relieved to find '... our father never was so well since I can remember; he has grown quite lusty ... He gets up to breakfast, eats supper, and never retires till after ten. Keep his mind at rest, and I do not fear but he will live these many years'. He goes on to mention his plans of returning to France 'to many charming women, but no charming woman will return with me.'

Recalled in March 1784, and given a new command in the *Boreas*, Nelson returned to the West Indies where he encountered the young wife of the Commissioner of Antigua, Mary Moutray. She captivated Nelson and his fellow officer Cuthbert Collingwood, both by her energy and wit, though she was not considered beautiful. Her husband, 40 years older and a retired Naval officer, provoked Nelson by flying his own pennant, not recognising him (Nelson) as the senior officer on station. Not withstanding their professional differences, the Moutrays gave the young captains the run of their house.

The old commissioner's health declined and the couple returned home, eventually to Bath in March 1785. Nelson, writing to his brother William, the Reverend Mr Nelson, said: 'I really am an April day; happy on her account, but truly grieved were I only to consider myself. Her equal I never saw in any country or in any situation. She always talks of you and hopes, if she comes within your reach, you will not fail to visiting her; for my dear friend has promised to make herself known. What an acquisition to any female to be acquainted with: what an example to take a pattern from' ... 'What a treasure of a woman'.

On the south aisle of Bath Abbey is a white marble tablet 'To the memory of John Moutray Esq. 28 years Post Captain and late commissioner of His Majesty's Navy at Antigua died November 22nd 1785. Her only son James Moutray, a Lieutenant R.N aged 21, whose godfather was Lord Hood, caught a fever while serving ashore at the siege of Calvi in Corsica, in 1793. Buried San Fiorenzo Italy'. It was Nelson who paid for the headstone. During this action Nelson lost the sight in his right eye. Collingwood, who had remained in contact with Mary Moutray, years later wrote to her of the sad loss of their friend Nelson at the Battle of Trafalgar in 1805. Mary Moutray left Bath and moved to live with relatives in Ireland, dying at the age of 88 in 1843.

A few months later, 1 January 1786, Nelson announced to his brother William that he was sitting next to the woman who is to be his wife. 'I am more than ever convinced of the propriety of my choice ... and her manners are of Mrs Moutray's'. The woman concerned was a widow, Frances Nesbit, with a young son, Josiah. She was the housekeeper and niece to the President of the Council of the Island of Nevis, Mr Herbert. Frances ('Fanny') Woolward's (her maiden name) family originated in Redland, Bristol. Her father, William Woolward Senior, was Justice for the Island of Nevis, and brother-in-law of the President of the island, John Herbert, for whom she worked when Nelson met her.

Fanny, as Nelson addressed her, married her first husband Josiah Nisbet, a doctor who had cared for her dying father; her mother died when she was only two. Josiah Nisbet's family came from Nevis but originated from Salisbury, Wiltshire. Soon after the birth of their son Josiah the family returned briefly to Salisbury where the doctor died in 1781. Fanny, without any immediate family, returned to Nevis with her young son to keep house for her uncle and care for his young sickly daughter.

For Nelson, Fanny, a year younger than him, was a good catch; her uncle John Herbert was a vocal supporter for Nelson's zealous enforcement of the 'Navigation Act', not popular with many of the local merchants, and promised to stand bail for him should the matter go to law. Nelson not only needed a wife but money. Writing to his uncle William Suckling he mentions the wealth of Mr Herbert of £20,000 and, should his daughter die, then the bulk would go to Fanny, but in the meantime he feels Mr Herbert would give her £200 a year but could Suckling give Nelson a £1000, or an annual amount of £100 to help the young couple get started? Mr Herbert died in 1793 leaving Nelson £4000, but it took a lot of badgering from Fanny to get the executors to pay up.

The couple married on 11 March 1787; Prince William Henry insisted on being their best man. Nelson described Frances, 'as an amiable woman, until I married her I never knew happiness'.

Prince William Henry, the Duke of Clarence and eventually King William IV, was introduced to Nelson in November 1782 by Lord Hood on board *Barfleur* in which the 17-year old prince served as a midshipman. Later Nelson was appointed William Henry's aide de camp while he was in the West Indies. The Duke was an early admirer of Nelson long before he was famous, and they were to remain lifelong friends. Nelson's posting drew to a close in December of that year; with peace being declared with France, he returned home.

Nelson soon visited Bath in January 1788 with his new wife, staying in his old lodgings at 2 Pierrepont Street as a base between their respective excursions to Exeter, Bristol or Plymouth; in Nelson's case to see the young Prince William Henry, and Fanny her relations. Her son, Josiah, had been farmed out to Nelson's brother the Reverend William Nelson of Hillborough in Norfolk to attend school, along with his own children. Describing himself as being in the best of health Nelson took the opportunity to take the waters in the present Pump Room overlooking the King's Bath, an integral part of the cure his father had depended on for so many years – a dose being a glass or two of the tepid water to three gallons a day! Writing from Bath to his old friend Captain Locker, Nelson said he was 'obliged by your kind enquiries about a house. I fear we must at present give up all thoughts of living so near London, for Mrs Nelson's lungs are so much affected by the smoke of London, that I cannot think of placing her in that situation'. Without a home of their own, they returned to Burnham Thorpe to live in the parsonage with Edmund Nelson for what was to be a long wait for Nelson's recall by the Admiralty.

Little is known of Nelson's activities beyond the fact that he dug a pond to the outline of his first command the brig *Badger* (still to be seen today over the wall of the Parsonage) and to 'study', read the London newspapers to glean the slightest news of hostilities being renewed. Desperate for a new command, Nelson wrote to the First Lord of the Admiralty, the second Earl Chatham, whose father, Pitt the Elder, had been the MP for Bath, and whose brother, William Pitt, 'The Younger', Prime Minister, to no avail. Even Admiral Lord Hood, his patron in the West Indies and now a Member of the Board of Admiralty, although sympathetic, could not oblige.

One curiosity was an appeal he made to the Duke of Clarence; ever conscious of the cost of living, it was an account on the required income for an agricultural worker and his family in Norfolk, highlighting their plight, and their gentlemen employers to recognise a need for a rise in wages, concluding that to survive on water alone on twopence a day is not tenable. Fanny, meanwhile, during the bitter winter months, would retire to her bed. Edmund developed a strong rapport with his daughter-in-law, and offered any help he could when Nelson returned to sea.

FANNY NELSON SEA WIDOW 1793-97

After five years of unemployment, 'on the beach', when hostilities were resumed with the French Nelson was given a new command, the *Agamemnon*, at Chatham in January 1793. Much of the crew were recruited in Norfolk, including two

It was at 17 New King Street that Fanny Nelson came to live as a 'sea widow' in 1794 as both Nelson and her son, Josiah Nesbit, had sailed in the *Agamemnon*. Here, in September three years later, Nelson returned, invalided home after the loss of his arm at Santa Cruz in 1797.

midshipmen, one of them being his step-son Josiah, who was unable to afford any other profession, and the other was William Hoste, the son of a nearby Norfolk parson at Titteshall, 16 miles from Burnham Thorpe. Unaccustomed to preparing for a naval officer's departure Fanny had omitted various necessary items, including the key to his bureau, but had included a keg of tongues and some poorly packed Norfolk hams and bacon, well rubbed after the long journey .

With Nelson's return to sea, Fanny accompanied her father-in-law to Bath, anything to escape those fierce Norfolk winters when, during much of the time, she took to her bed. Fanny spent a year in a round of visits that included Bath, but essentially she had no fixed address until she rented 17 New King Street, Bath, in 1794. The property became vacant with the death of the owner, Mrs Searle. This was convenient for both Fanny to be near her relatives and friends from the West Indies in Bristol, and for her father-in-law to visit from Norfolk. Nelson was perfectly happy with her choice of Bath, but as yet could not afford a house of his own. Fanny, aware as to how careful she needed to be, reasoned in a letter to Nelson her choice; the house cost £90 a year to rent as opposed to £160 a year in Gay Street, 'the higher you go the dearer'. Fanny was not to be dissuaded having been told, 'this situation was too low. Bath is so hot in the summer and so stinking that very few remain in it'. A later tenant, Mrs Piozzi (Mrs Thrale, a friend of Dr Johnson) in 1814 described the lodgings as 'dingy'.

Mrs Nelson had brought a maid with her from Norfolk, Bett Thurlow, but she left, bad tempered and complaining that Bath did not agree with her; and there was 'Will' her man-servant, fond of the bottle, who helped to look after her father-in-law Edmund. She remarked that 'the servants in this town [Bath] is, I am sorry to say very bad'. A new maidservant was found, from Torbay, who had worked for a Portuguese merchant, and would add a little more sophistication to the household.

Bath was almost unique for attracting everyone, either for pleasure, the cure, or both, and one of the principal resorts outside London. At some point anyone of note passed through Bath including politicians and naval officers. Useful to an ambitious young naval officer, it could not have been a better place for his wife, a chance to observe and socialise, and report back to Nelson in the Mediterranean.

Occasionally Mrs Nelson would be persuaded by her father-in-law to attend dances, though she was apparently not particularly enthusiastic and all too aware of the potential extra expense for a suitable outfit. However, several acquaintances of Nelson's from the West Indies would ask Fanny to dine, and naval officers back from the Mediterranean would seek, and reassure her of the health of Josiah and Nelson. Any intelligence, such as naval gossip from Bath, Fanny passed on in her weekly letters.

By now aged 34 years, Nelson was hungry to make up for the time he had spent ashore, and took every opportunity to be in the thick of the action. Lord Hood, Commander-in-Chief in the Mediterranean, knew of Nelson's capabilities from the West Indies, and sent him on special detachments, one to Naples, to get reinforcements for the occupation of Toulon. Here he met Emma Hamilton for the first time in September 1793. Losing Toulon, the British were briefly involved with the occupation of Corsica. Clearing the island of the French, Nelson distinguished himself in the assault on Calvi where, struck by debris, he lost effective sight in his right eye, and later he besieged Bastia. These exploits did not reassure Fanny when he wrote, 'I am convinced you feel interested in very action of my life; and my exultation in victory is two fold, knowing that you partake of it. Only recollect that a brave man dies but once, a coward all his long life'.

Samuel, First Viscount Hood (1724-1816) was Nelson's patron whom he first encountered in the West Indies, and who introduced him to the Duke of Clarence. Hood was Nelson's commander in the Mediterranean in 1793 when, after five years 'on the beach', Nelson was able to prove himself in the abortive occupation of Corsica. Hood and his wife comforted Fanny Nelson when in Bath and he was chief mourner at Nelson's funeral in 1806. Warwick Leadlay Gallery, Greenwich.

Lord Hood, as Commander-in-Chief, exhausted by these operations, was given leave to return to England, and came to Bath with his wife, to stay at 16 Milsom Street. Encouraged by Nelson, within two weeks of their arrival in December 1794 Fanny paid them a visit, and was clearly distressed at the absence of her husband and begged his Lordship to influence her husband's early recall. Driven to distraction she complained to her husband that the effect it all had on her health, much to Nelson's surprise since it was all in the line of duty. Fanny pressed home the lack of recognition and the necessity of a pension for the loss of his eye. Lord Hood and his wife were most gracious, entertaining and visiting Fanny, inviting her to Christmas lunch, and trying to persuade her that Nelson would soon be home. In the company of Lord and Lady Hood, Fanny was introduced to fellow officers from the Mediterranean, such as the Commissioner in Corsica, Captain John Inglefield, Dr Harness, Surgeon to the Fleet (who signed the certificate for the loss of Nelson's eye on board *Victory*), and Admiral Cosby (third in command in the Mediterranean), all of whom spoke of their high regard for Nelson. Writing to Nelson, Lord Hood, said of his wife, that they were 'received with every mark of affection and said all that would gratify an affectionate wife'.

Lord Hood's successor, Admiral Hotham, dithered, calling off the pursuit of a French squadron off Toulon, whilst Nelson tenaciously continued the chase, eventually capturing the *Ça Ira* (92 guns and crew of 1300). Nelson made an impression in the Mediterranean. Receiving a letter addressed 'Nelson Genoa'; the correspondent was asked how he expected it to be delivered, 'there is but one Horatio Nelson in the world', he replied. .

Fanny wrote as much as she could on what she felt her husband wanted to hear at least once a week, sending her letters either through the Admiralty, by 'packet' or more reliably via naval officers either on Nelson's ship or in the Fleet. Her response to the ladies of Bath she remarks, 'the ladies of quality have fashion in their mode of speaking, laughing, or smiling at every word they say which I don't like'. Her encounter with the Viceroy of Corsica's wife, Lady Elliot, staying in Bath, a good friend of Nelson's reported as follows; ' the day I returned her visit though she received me as if I was honoured ... Lady E had forgot she was not the person she was at Corsica, however she is mistaken, it is not in her power by her acquaintance to honour your wife, and so little do I covert the acquaintance of the fashionable that I would rather shun it.'

The Reverend Edmund Nelson wrote in contrast rather sage letters about the rest of the family, reflecting on Nelson's progress, the concerns of the day, often with a postscript on the state of the harvest with a view to the rate of tithe for the church. On Nelson's promotion to Colonel of Marines, an indirect pension for his injuries which paid £400 per year, though proud of his son, Edmund intones, 'you must subordinate to your opinion, interest and reputation.'

Apart from writing letters, Fanny took up learning the piano she had bought for £25, attending church, and looking after Edmund Nelson. She apologised for the lack of talent learning music at Nelson's expense but put in plenty of practice. Fanny was ever cautious over the money she spent, Nelson reminded her that she should spend the interest from the legacy from her uncle, Mr Herbert, (who had died just prior to Nelson returning to sea) and to apply to his agents Marsh and Creed should she need more.

Reporting on the family, Maurice Nelson, who worked in the Navy Office (Somerset House) kept in touch and forwarded any news: while the Reverend William was conspicuous by his absence having a 'living' in Hillborough in Norfolk,

Leghorn miniature of Nelson painted at the request of his wife who had heard that Italy was the place to have a portrait painted. Although a poor likeness, it was a treasured possession of Fanny in a locket and shown as a treat to the favoured few. National Maritime Museum, Greenwich.

Suckling is sinking into drink and tries to run a shop in Norfolk, and Nelson's sisters, Kitty Matcham and Susannah Bolton, are occupied with their young families. The frustration and impact of war and a shortage of grain on the population is reflected in Edmund's observation, that the cry seems 'Bread and Peace' !

Fanny continued to live in Bath throughout the time Nelson spent in the Mediterranean – her 'widowhood' as Edmund called it; she became more concerned for the return of her husband and son. Away from home, his ship in dock undergoing repairs in Leghorn, in the winter of 1794 Nelson is said to have had a liaison, not an affair, with an opera singer, Adelaide Correglia, to the surprise of some officers. Captain Fremantle notes; 'Dined at Nelson's and his dolly'. Fanny had heard that Italy was the place to have a portrait painted; Nelson commissioned a local Leghorn artist to paint a miniature portrait; although not a good likeness it became a treasured possession of Fanny.

After three years at sea the strain was beginning to tell and there was much discussion about acquiring a house. Nelson's preference was somewhere quiet in the Norfolk countryside, but as long 'as it is a real fixed home'. Fanny was also exhausted in anticipation of his return. Edmund described their life in Bath: 'I have not been to one party this winter nor drink tea from home, Mrs N. has had a bad cold, and she is sometimes a little low in spirit, for we do not go abroad, we see but few and only hear of the Gaiety and Luxury of this place'.

The British withdrew from the Mediterranean by the end of 1796 to their base in Lisbon. With the evacuation of the island of Elba Nelson was promoted to Commodore and joined the *Captain*.

On 14 February 1797, Sir John Jervis's fleet of 14 ships encountered off Cape St

Vincent on the Atlantic coast, a Spanish fleet of 30 ships escorting a South American convoy. A disorderly engagement ensued, Commodore Nelson distinguished himself by breaking the Line and, in so doing, captured with his 'patent bridge' two Spanish ships of the line, the *San Josef*, 100 guns, and *San Nicolas*, 112 guns.

News reached Bath in early March of what became known as the Battle of Cape St Vincent. Everyone talked of Nelson, Lady Saumarez, whose husband was in the action, wrote: 'Com. Nelson's conduct was above praise', and ran to tell Fanny. The city of Bath was hungry for news. Edmund exclaimed, 'the name and services of Nelson have sounded throughout the City of Bath from the common ballad singer to the public theatre'. At Denner's off Bond Street in Bath, was ' a depiction of vessels in motion and as large and real' that could be viewed at a shilling (5p) a time, and of Jervis' victory, 'Here is seen the true value of seamen, who after hard services are all too often neglected'.

Not mentioned in the official dispatch, Nelson produced his own account witnessed by his Captain, Ralph Miller and Lieutenant Berry who lead the boarding parties. This account was later published in 1799 in the *Naval Chronicle*. Later Fanny bought a copy of Colonel Drinkwater's eye-witness account of the battle, which she approved of as it did her dear husband justice.

Nelson was promoted to Rear Admiral and created a Knight of the Order of the Bath, at his own request; he felt he could not afford a peerage. He is quoted as saying to Colonel Drinkwater, 'he wished to bear about his person some honorary distinction, to attract the public eye, and mark his professional services'. Fanny's reaction was, ' I rejoice you have at last begun to be noticed in a proper manner, the Ribbon will not satisfy me. I expect they will give you a handsome pension, if they do not then you must ask for it.' Josiah Nesbit was made a Lieutenant.

In May, Fanny wrote of the mutinies within the Fleet and her anxiety; she had received the news from Mrs Bickerton whose husband, Rear Admiral Bickerton, had been driven from his ship, later to be returned whilst at Spithead. The newly promoted Captain Berry came to Bath with gifts of two seascapes, some Roman pearls and a silk handkerchief from Mrs Freemantle, wife of one of Nelson's captains, to recount events to Fanny and Edmund and reassure them of the health of Nelson and Josiah. Once Nelson's knighthood and promotion were gazetted Nelson addressed his letters to Lady Nelson.

Meanwhile a well-connected parson, Dixon Hoste from Godwick near Burnham Thorpe, paid Edmund and Fanny a visit while in Bath, as his son was one of Nelson's young gentlemen in the *Agamemnon*. This was not a welcome visit as Edmund was all too aware that their lifestyle was rather plain for this ambitious country parson whose friendship and 'living' was provided by the Coke family (Earls of Leicester) of Holkham, and who had considerable political interests in

Norfolk at the time. However, Nelson was very complimentary of Midshipman Hoste's progress, writing long letters to his father, on their deployment.

After the excitement had died down following the Battle of Cape St Vincent, Nelson wrote to his wife that he would not be writing any letters for a while as he would be on a special detachment, with the approval of his commander Sir John Jervis, later Earl St Vincent. Nelson was dispatched to blockade Cadiz, and later to make an abortive raid on Santa Cruz on Tenerife in July 1797, in the vain attempt to capture a Spanish treasure ship. On the second attempt, as Nelson approached in his cutter, he was shot in the right arm above the elbow and fortunately saved by the tourniquet applied by his stepson Josiah Nisbet. Back on board his ship *Theseus* Nelson's arm was amputated by surgeon Thomas Eshelby, assisted by his mate Louis Ronicet (a French Royalist surgeon from Toulon who had left in 1793).

Fanny's worst fears were confirmed when, reassured in a letter from Sir John Jervis, Nelson's commander, that, although wounded but not dangerously, he would return home with all speed.

VICTORY AND RENOWN 1797 AND LAST VISIT IN 1798

Nelson landed in Portsmouth from the *Seahorse*, on 1 September and struck his flag on 3 September. He set off immediately for Bath and 17 New King Street to be re-united with his wife after four years separation. The local paper announced, 'arrived in this city on Sunday evening in good health and spirits to the great joy of Lady Nelson and his venerable father'. In the local papers the Corporation of Bath welcomed Nelson's safe return and swift recovery.

Prior to his arrival Fanny had received a scribbled note by his left hand, not having received any warning of his wound, and deciphered it with the help of Nelson's sister Susannah Bolton; this only added to her anxiety. Returning from church Fanny, Edmund and Susannah were roused by the arrival of a coach and the familiar voice of Nelson, who was accompanied by Louis Ronicet, surgeon's mate in the *Theseuss* to dress his wound.

The amputated arm required daily dressing, and Nelson took opium at night to relieve the pain. He described to a family friend, "as to myself, I suppose I was getting well too fast, for I am beset with a Physician, Surgeon and Apothecary ... and to say the truth, am suffering much pain with some fever.' For his physician he consulted the renowned Dr Falconer at his address, 6 Bladud Buildings, the senior physician of the Mineral Hospital who, understandably not an expert in amputation, recommended that Nelson see a London surgeon better qualified than he; consultation cost a guinea. Impressed by his patient, Falconer's wife later related to Fanny that, had he been single he would have signed up to join Nelson. His surgeon, Mr Nicolls at 14 Queen Square, quite close to the Nelson lodgings, dressed the wound daily while Nelson was in Bath. His apothecary was Nelson's former landlord Joseph Spry of 2 Pierrepont Street.

The wound, according to the practice by which Nelson's arm was amputated, was to leave the 'long silk ligatures hanging out of the wound after the operation, so that as suppuration took place and the ligatures separated by necrosis and granulation, they could be pulled out the second or fourth weeks' says Surgeon Commander Pugh in *Nelson and his Surgeons*. There is a lot of discussion as to the best technique, with various opinions offered, suffice it to say that, thankfully, Nelson survived and was a testament to the surgeon Thomas Eshelby and subsequent after-care.

Fanny at last could nurse her beloved husband, who ensured she could dress his wound and act as his secretary. Writing with his left hand to Earl St Vincent following the raid on Santa Cruz, he described his lot: ' A left-handed Admiral will never again be considered useful, therefore the sooner I get to a very humble cottage the better, and make room for a better man to serve the State'. To give the re-united couple some privacy, his father Edmund had arranged lodgings in Charles Street just around the corner now that New King Street was getting quite full. Along with his sister, William Nelson hurried over from Norfolk to see his brother, as announced in the *Bath Chronicle*. Nelson wrote with his left hand a letter of acceptance to the Bath Corporation for the Freedom of the City, and strangely an editorial appears in the *Chronicle* addressed to 'Nurses, Parents and Guardians a petition by Nelson's Left hand, that you are not a lost cause with only one arm'. Earlier in the year the flag officers at the Battle of Cape St Vincent were made Freemen of the City: Admiral Sir John Jervis, Vice Admiral Waldegrave, Vice Admiral Thompson, Rear Admiral Parker and Commodore Nelson. This entitled them all to a pension of £25 per year. Nelson was offered the Freedom of many cities, such as Bristol but, as with Bath, never collected it.

Nelson spent two weeks in Bath, before setting out for London. He had an audience with the King, being presented by Admiral Earl Howe, to be invested with 'the red sash' of a Knight Companion of the Order of the Bath, and he received the Freedom of the City of London from John Wilkes of 'Liberty' fame. Now famous, he was much in demand by artists, in particular he sat for the painter Lemuel Abbot and the sculptor Lawrence Gahagan. He attended a service of Thanksgiving at St Paul's Cathedral with the Royal Family for the recent victories at sea. By the middle of December his wound had sufficiently healed for the Royal College of Surgeons

The 'Crystal Palace', formerly 10 and 11 Abbey Green. Here Nelson and his wife came to stay for the last time together in Bath to escape the fumes of London for two weeks before his return to sea in the *Vanguard*. The only relic from that period is the fireplace in the bar to the left of the entrance. Nelson would have also known the Plane tree in the centre of the Green.

to pass him fit to be appointed to a new vessel, and he was eager to rejoin John Jervis, now ennobled as Earl St Vincent, and return to sea. He wrote to his Captain, Edward Berry, to 'speedily marry or Mrs Berry will have little of your company.'

The topic that had dominated Nelson's correspondence with Fanny while at sea was to fix somewhere of their own to live. Susannah Bolton's brother-in-law Sam had found a suitable property which Fanny and Nelson drove from London to view. The 'little cottage', in fact Roundwood Farm comprising nearly 60 acres, near Ipswich, was quickly bought by Nelson for £2000. The papers were signed in November 1797 and witnessed by Captain Berry, but the tenant still had six months of tenancy to run before they could take possession of the house.

In 1798 the smoke of London proved too much for Fanny, and so they returned to Bath in January for a two week holiday while awaiting the preparation of the *Vanguard*. They lodged in 11 Abbey Green (now part of the Crystal Palace public house); the proprietor was a Mrs Norton who charged 10s 6d (52½p) a week and 5s 6d (27½p) for servants. The only remnant from this period is possibly the

Georgian grate in the Lounge bar of the Crystal Palace. The magnificent 'plane' tree in the centre of the square Nelson would have known.

The Nelsons took full advantage of the pleasures of Bath. Nelson writes of the pleasure of attending the Theatre Royal, Orchard Street. Taking Earl Lansdowne's place in Mr Palmer's box, he wrote, 'his Lordship did not tell me all its charms, that generally some of the most handsomest ladies in Bath are partakers in the box, and was I a bachelor I would not answer for being tempted; but I am possessed of everything which is valuable in a wife, I have no occasion to think beyond a pretty face'. Nelson goes on to mention how, although there was a Fund for the present war, he felt his contribution would be to 'debar myself of many comforts to serve my Country, and I expect great consolation every time I cut a slice of salt beef instead of mutton'. Other attractions were the Assembly Rooms to play cards, concerts or Balls, but much of the time was spent paying social calls and catching up on relatives.

Across the way from their lodgings lived Admiral Samuel Barrington at 1 Abbey Green, a good friend of both Nelson and Fanny, who they knew from their time in the West Indies. Barrington was a contemporary of John Jervis, the two of them as young officers had surveyed all the major naval ports of the Baltic, North Sea and Mediterranean. Samuel Barrington's cousin, Mr Daines Barrington, a naturalist, was instrumental in the Admiralty's expedition to the Arctic of the bomb vessels *Carcass* and *Racehorse*, when Nelson had served as coxswain in his Captain's gig.

Little is recorded in their correspondence of their activities, the stay lasted three weeks. Fanny returned later to Bath for a further few months staying with Edmund to sort out their effects that were held in storage in Bath at Wiltshire's 'near the old Bridge', for removal to their new home in Ipswich. Her household consisted of, 'an old Catholic cook near 60 years of age, a girl of fourteen and Will' . She dined with Captain Phillip and his wife, who had commanded the first fleet to Australia, both good friends of the Nelsons. Edmund sent Nelson items down on the wagon to Portsmouth from the Angel Inn, Bath.

In March 1798 Nelson returned to Portsmouth and his new command, *Vanguard*. In a letter to Fanny he tells her to check the weather vane on the roof of St Mary's chapel in Queen Square (now demolished but it stood on the south-west corner; a small colonnaded monument now marks the spot) to see whether he had sailed. Departure delayed through contrary winds, Nelson checked his wife's packing which, much to his frustration, did not seem to match the lists accompanying his chests. He was short of socks, stocks and small amounts of gold, and in fact had to send ashore for more clothes which, much to his disdain, were double the price of the originals. Eventually, at the beginning of April, he set sail for Portugal.

Neptune and Britannia in Neptune's chariot was a popular motif at the time. This was produced by Ackerman and appeared on Nelson's coffin. It is an example of what might have accompanied the display on Mr Normus's auction rooms in Walcot Street during the celebrations in October 1798 at the news of the victory over the French fleet at the Battle of the Nile.

The next Bath heard of Nelson's exploits, as in London, was in October 1798, with the news of the victory on 1 August at the Battle of the Nile and the defeat of the French Fleet. A collection was made for orphans and widows, reported in the *Bath Journal* of 15 October, the Guildhall and lending libraries: Bull's, Baratt's, Meyler, Bally's, Marshall's, Brown's, Hazard's, amounting to £453.9s.4d. In Bath the celebrations were suitably patriotic and reported in November: 'At the particular request of the Magistrates, the inhabitants did not illuminate their houses on the evening of Wednesday last, but the joy that displayed itself by every other means is not to be described – gilt laurels, elegant ribbons with appropriate mottos, appeared in every bosom. The mayor gave an elegant cold collation at the hall with a general invitation to the whole corps of Bath volunteers and to the inhabitants at large, when the greatest harmony prevailed to a later hour. The mayor's toast was given with the most enthusiastic bursts of approbation and loyalty

1. Pierrepoint Street

No. 2   Nelson stayed 1781
        Nelson to visit father 1784
        Nelson and wife Fanny 1788
No. 9   Edmund Nelson (father)
        1781

2. Orchard Street

Masonic Hall site of the original
Theatre Royal (1766-1805)
Nelson attended in 1798

3. Abbey Green

No. 10, 11 'Crystal Palace' pub.
On this site Nelson and Fanny
stayed in No. 11 in 1798

4. Pump Room

Here Edmund Nelson regularly
drank the waters, as did Nelson as
part of his cure in 1781.

5. Bath Abbey

Commemorative plaques to Nelson
contemporaries (see inset plan):
1. Palmer 2. Phillip 3. Shirley
4. Bickerton 5. Cosby 6. Gardner
7. Connolly 8. Hargood 9. Duff
10. Moutray

6. Cross Bath Bath St.

7. Trim Street

No. 5   Wolfe House
Here Nelson's hero, General Wolfe
stayed in the 1750s

8. Beaufort Square

Theatre Royal entrance of
1805 railings said to commemorate
Battle of Trafalgar

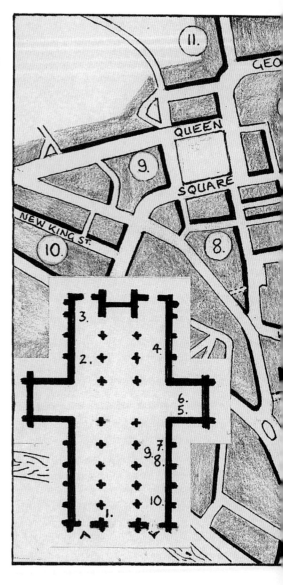

PLAN

Showing places associated with

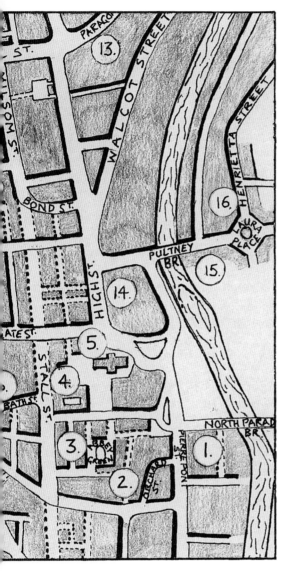

9. Queen's Square
No. 5 Lord and Lady Hood 1795
No. 14 Surgeon Nicolls 1797
No. 25 Admiral Hargood 1812
South west corner site of
St. Mary's Chapel

10. New King Street
Anne Nelson said to live in 1783
No. 17 Frances Nelson 1794-7
No. 10 Frances Nelson 1805

11. Gay Street
No. 2 Admiral Edward Berry 1783
No. 8 Dr Woodward
      Nelson's doctor in 1781

12. Milsom Street
No. 16 Lord Hood
Octagon Chapel, Fanny attended.
Watson's Milliners where Nelson
sisters apprenticed.

13. Bladud Buildings
No. 6 Dr Falconer examined
      Nelson 1797

14. Guildhall
Victoria Art Gallery

15. Argyle Street
No. 8 Jervis Earl St. Vincent
      stayed with sister

16. Henrietta Street
No. 20 Admiral Mark Robinson,
      Nelson's Captain in the
      Worcester 1776.
      Thomas Pitt Robinson,
      midshipman at Trafalgar.

BATH
on. Inset a plan of Bath Abbey

"The hero of the day our brave fellow citizen Admiral Horatio Nelson".' At the New Assembly Rooms Miss Cantelo, as part of her performance, concluded with a piece she had composed, 'Lord Nelson's March' which had been adapted for two harps.

The same month news of Admiral John Borlases Warren's victory over the French fleet in Bantry Bay (Ireland) was relayed in passing 'en route' to London. This caused a general illumination of Bath celebrating the victories of Nelson and Warren and was reported in the *Bath Journal*. The White Hart Inn had full length portraits of the successful admirals with 'Howe' in the centre and pyramids of colour lamps either side, with other inns covered in festoons; the King's Arms had a transparency of *Vanguard* with the motto 'May the British Fleet prove invincible and success to His Majesty' arms'; the Elephant and Castle had a portrait of Nelson and the wooden walls of Old England with Warren and *Victory*. Individuals such as Mr Bretson in New King Street spelt the words Nelson and Warren in coloured lamps. One of the more impressive was Mr Normus (auctioneer) of Walcot Street, who displayed Neptune in his chariot and a distant view of the hostile fleet with the inscription;

> May dauntless Neptune guard our favoured isle -
> May England flourish and commerce smile-
> Let no invading traitor dare boast-
> While Duncan Nelson Warren be our toast.

There were many other examples in a long list.

LADY NELSON AND THE NELSON FAMILY

Lady Nelson moved into her new home, built five years earlier, at Roundwood near Ipswich despite the rumour that Suffolk houses might be requisitioned for barracks to counter the threatened invasion. Nelson persisted in calling it his cottage, yet it was a reasonable sized house, with a large barn, a cow house and other offices, and a well-planted garden with roughly 50 acres of productive land. It was a step up from the rented house in New King Street, Bath. For Fanny this was a new experience and required careful attention to provide the right impression of a gentleman's home, from the wine cellar to ordering a chaise at a cost of £320, and carriage horses. She struggled with the expense of it all.

Relatively few remedial works were needed; her new footman from Bath proved a success, while she retained her servant Will and maid Kitty. This was the beginning in providing a home fit for a gentleman. For company, various nieces went to stay: Charlotte Nelson, the Bolton girls and Fanny also had the

Nelson depicted full length before the burning of the town of Santa Cruz, Tenerife. It is from a portrait by Lemuel Abbot engraved by Barnard. Its delivery to Lady Nelson was delayed by Barnard borrowing it, which was only half length, to produce this image, and thus excluded it from exhibition at the Royal Academy. A copy of this print was presented to Dr Falconer at Nelson's behest, whom he had consulted when in Bath with the loss of his arm.

companionship of Louisa, Captain Berry's wife. At last they had a home of their own, but cold and damp winters necessitated her visits to take the waters of Bath, often meeting Edmund, or Bristol friends, and sometimes travel to London.

Fanny went to the Royal Academy to see Abbot's portrait of Nelson, but was disappointed in only finding the white marble bust by Lawrence Gahagan that Nelson had sat for at the end of the previous year. The Gahagan family did well over the years producing plaster casts of this bust -- his son Lucius established a studio in Walcot Street, Bath. The centre-piece of the new house was a three-quarter length portrait of Nelson by Lemuel Abbot. In the ensuing years he was to paint around 40 portraits before being overtaken by madness. Fanny described the painting as 'my companion, my sincere friend in your absence'. Edmund was delighted with the likeness but delivery was delayed by the creation of a mezzotint (engraving) version by an artist called Barnard, extending the image full length before the flaming town of Santa Cruz. This was common practice at the time, popularising the subject as well as the artist. With public recognition, so the clamour grew for new portraits of which there was a very limited supply; by now Nelson was 40 years old and the only portrait had been that by Rigaud, 20 years earlier. Nelson subscribed for ten prints, Abbot says twenty. The cost of proofs and copies came to £18. It was published again on three occasions, after the Battles of the Nile, Copenhagen, and Trafalgar, and was hugely popular. Nelson asked Fanny to present one of the prints to Dr Falconer who had given him a medical examination of his arm in 1797. Lord Hood also received a copy. Fanny describes in one of her letters how another artist, Daniel Orme, a historical painter to the King, had been financially very successful with his engraving of the Rear Admiral.

Earl St Vincent, Commander-in-Chief in the Mediterranean, detached Nelson with his own squadron back to the Mediterranean to blockade and observe the activities of the French fleet in Toulon. Without frigates he was unable to reconnoitre, and the French managed to give him the slip. A desperate search found the French fleet at anchor off Aboukir at the mouth of the Nile. Sighted at four in the afternoon Nelson attacked despite the advance of nightfall and soundly defeated the French. Although wounded by a splinter striking his head, he reassured Fanny that he would be home by November.

At Roundwood Fanny complained of the lack of company, but with victory at the 'Nile' she again was in demand and was presented to the Queen. The *Bath Chronicle* reported that in Ipswich Lady Nelson attended a Ball and Supper, her host being Admiral Hughes, accompanied by Edmund Nelson in honour of the Battle of the Nile. Diverted by the ecstatic welcome in Naples by the enthusiastic Emma, Lady Hamilton, Nelson had to endure another two years in the Mediterranean. As the

Frances Lady Nelson, a pencil and water-colour portrait by Henry Edridge after Nelson had left her. Fanny's continued devotion is shown by the bust of Nelson on the table. She remained devoted to Nelson's father, Edmund, and was his constant companion during her visits to Bath. This was said to be the reason for Nelson not visiting his dying father in Bath in 1802.

'Hero of the Nile', he was plied with every honour, created a Baron of the Nile and, distracted, his correspondence with Fanny waned.

A year later he was created the Duke of Bronte and given an estate in the shadow of Etna, for evacuating the Royal Family from Naples to Sicily. The estate accrued £2000 per year which he diligently apportioned on paper to his family, but nothing much came of it. The estate passed down through his niece Charlotte, remaining in the Bridport family until 1981.

Fanny returned to Bath in mid-November 1799 with the Rector instead of spending the winter in Lisbon as recommended by her doctor, a suggestion not welcomed by Nelson. Eventually Nelson returned from Naples overland to England in the company of the Hamiltons, landing in Yarmouth in November 1800. A misunderstanding caused Nelson to miss his wife at their new home, Roundwood, the only time he visited the property, meanwhile his wife Fanny awaited him in the lodgings she had rented in Bond Street, London. The encounter was not a happy one mainly due to Nelson's infatuation with Emma (she was seven months pregnant with Nelson's child).

Nelson's time on his return to England was spent entirely with the Hamiltons, Christmas was spent with William Beckford (Hamilton's nephew) at the impressive Fonthill Abbey near Salisbury in Wiltshire. He then returned to his wife in London. Exasperated by the continual adulation of Lady Hamilton prompted Fanny to demand Nelson make a choice. He chose to leave his wife of 13 years in February 1801, paying her half his salary on the understanding they had no further contact and that he had no cause for any complaint for her actions. Roundwood was quickly sold in March 1801.

Nelson, anxious to return to sea, found that Fanny had failed again as an officer's wife in preparing his sea chests. Dispatched at considerable cost (£100), Nelson found them full of useless household items, only a proportion of clothing, and one of them stuffed with green tea! Fanny apologised and blamed the servants. She was devastated by the separation and tried in vain to get Nelson to return.

The dilemma for the Nelson family was the continued close friendship Fanny had with her father-in-law. Visiting Merton, Nelson and Emma Hamilton's new home in Wimbledon, bought in 1801, Edmund remained loyal to the last to Fanny, who visited him on his death-bed in Pulteney Street, Bath, in April 1802. Edmund in his discourse with Nelson and speaking of Emma, made his loyalty clear however; knowing of the Hamilton's taste for cream cheese, he sent them two or three of Bath manufacture. Nelson refused to see his dying father just in case he encountered Fanny.

Fanny continued to visit Bath primarily for her health and, at 14 Sydney Parade, almost as she arrived in Bath in November 1805, she received news from Lord

Barham, First Lord of the Admiralty, of the victory at Trafalgar and the death of Nelson in October. Admiral William Cornwallis, an old friend of the Nelson's from the West Indies, came to visit her. Cornwallis in 1781 had dissuaded Nelson from going to the hospital in Jamaica, which he described as a 'waiting room for the cemetery'. Fanny appears to have spent most of the year in the City, one of her nieces wrote of having seen her looking very old, having recovered from an illness that required two physicians to attend her.

Fanny received a pension of £2000 after Trafalgar while Nelson's sisters received £10,000. As a token of their esteem the 'Patriotic Fund' presented her with a silver vase (described as 'a vase of the value of £500 ornamented with emblematical devices and inscriptions, of the transcendent and heroic achievements of the late Lord Nelson') which ended up on Edward VII's yacht. The Bolton twins, despite having stayed with Fanny in Ipswich, wrote unkindly of her, while Nelson's brother William, along with his wife and daughter Charlotte, also visited. Fanny wrote of their visit while in Bath: 'I received them, they were much affected, and I think they have received some satisfaction from a shake of my hand'. William was created an Earl and given Trafalgar House, Standlynch near Salisbury, by a grateful nation, part of which was designed by John Wood the Younger of Bath, and a handsome pension paid until 1947.

Fanny 's last recorded visit to Bath was in 1815, and various contemporaries of Nelson such as Admiral Hotham and Earl St Vincent came to visit her. Fanny eventually went to live with her son Josiah's family at 8 The Beacon, Exmouth. Josiah married Fanny's god-daughter, and companion, Frances Evans, spending much time sailing around England and France; they had three surviving daughters. Without the patronage of his step-father Josiah was not given another command in the Navy after 1800, instead he made a large fortune trading on the Stock Market in London and Paris, on the Bourse in Paris dealing in 'rentes' (government stocks). He died in Paris in 1830, predeceasing his mother who died aged 73 in 1831. Both are buried at Littleham, Exmouth.

THE CITY OF BATH NELSON REMEMBERED

News of the defeat of the Danish fleet at the Battle of Copenhagen, reached Bath on 22 April 1801 and was reported in the *Bath Journal*; a collection was made for the widows and orphans, with a donation from the Corporation of £50 plus approximately £100 collected in all.

News of the Battle of Trafalgar on 21 October 1805, reached the City on 6 November with the official dispatch published in the *London Gazette*. A lengthy obituary written for the *Bath Chronicle* was very much in the heroic style and signed W.F. The Common Hall of the Corporation voted 100 guineas for the relief of Sailors and Marines, widows and orphans. A book was opened for the Patriotic Fund with collections in Church amounting to £915 6s 2d of the £120,000 collected nationally.

Bath Abbey	£92	2	0
St James Church	£51	7	2
St Michael's Church	£27	8	0
Walcot	£37	1	0
Bathwick	£5	13	6
Christchurch	£53	6	3
Laura Chapel	£166	18	0
Octagon	£12	14	6
St John's Chapel	£7	13	0
All Saints Chapel	£39	13	11
Kensington Chapel	£12	10	6
Lady Huntingdon Chapel	£25	16	0
Moravian	£7	2	0
Argyle Chapel	£24	2	0
Catholic Chapel	£17	4	1
Unitarian	£38	19	6
Widcombe Church	£16	9	0
Casual Collection	£9	6	0
Total	**£915**	**6**	**2**

At the New Theatre Royal, a one act musical tribute, 'Nelson's Glory', that had been performed in the Theatre Royal, Covent Garden, played for a week. Characters included Tom Tackle, Volunteer, Caleb Quotum, Farmer, Excise man, Blacksmith and Barber, concluding with Rule Britannia and view of the Triumphant Fleet. An additional verse had been written for Rule Britannia by Mr Ashley of Bath:

> Again the loud trump of fame
> Proclaims Britannia rules the Main;
> Whilst sorrow whisper's NELSON's name,
> And mourns the gallant Victor slain.
> Rule, brave Britons, rule the main,
> Avenge the god-like Hero slain

At the Assembly Rooms Mr Rauzzini, a musical impresario, to start the new season of subscription concerts, performed a 'Dirge for Lord Nelson' written by the Reverend Bowles and set to music by Rauzzini:

> Toll Nelson's Knell! a soul more brave
> Ne' er triumph'd on green sea wave!
> Sad o'er the Hero's honoured grave
>   Toll Nelson's Knell
> The ball of Death unerring flew;
> His cheque has lost its ardent hue,
> He sinks, amid the gallant Crew!
>   Toll Nelson's Knell
> Yet lift, brave Chief, thy dying eyes
> Hark! loud huzzas round thee arise
> Aloft the flag of conquest flies
>   The Day is won!
> The day is won – peace to the brave
> But whilst the joyous streamers wave
> We'll think upon the Victor's Grave
>   Peace to the Brave.

An anonymous letter to the Editor of the *Bath Chronicle* related that success came with Nelson's careful care of his men; wine instead of spirits, avoiding harbours, encouraging music and dance ...'.

A notice appeared in the *Bath Chronicle* for December 1805:

> 'in consequence of an application having been made to me for the purpose of promoting a subscription to defray the expense of erecting a Naval monument in Memory of the Late illustrious Hero, Admiral Viscount Nelson a meeting will be holden at the Guildhall on Friday 6th December, at Twelve-o-clock at noon to take the same into consideration
> Charles Phillott Mayor.'

The proposal had been for a monument in Laura Place or the Circus, but nothing happened, no one turned up for the meeting!

The Day of Thanksgiving in December 1805 produced several sermons committed to print and later advertised for a shilling (5p) in the paper or part of a bigger collection of sermons available in book form. All the collections made were to be distributed for the relief of seamen, soldiers, marines and volunteers, and to widows, orphans and relatives of those killed.

Local militia paraded, feasted on beef and fired a 'feu de joie' to celebrate Trafalgar, while toasts were drunk by various groups, like the Harmonic Dinner held at the White Hart, which reported: 'Toast given to the immortal memory of Lord Nelson and every British Hero who fell in the Battle of Trafalgar', drunk with the members upstanding, and to 'Lord Collingwood and the surviving heroes', drunk three times.

The official day of mourning was 9 January 1806 when Nelson was buried in the crypt of St Paul's Cathedral, London. In Bath, the muffled church bells tolled throughout the day, patriotic sermons were delivered (William Jay's of Argyle Chapel was later published); in the evening the Pump Room band played dirges. On the balcony of the Theatre Royal a gong struck throughout the day resembling the bell of St Paul's. Mr Weeks the manager, dressed in a sailor's uniform, spoke through a speaking trumpet to the assembled crowd of the terrific sacrifice Nelson had made. In the Guildhall, displayed by special permission of the Mayor, was a model of a mausoleum to celebrate Nelson and his victories by an 'architect of the city', J. Lowder, 'with a skill and taste truly classic and professional'. It was advertised in the *Bath Journal*, that John Boydell & Co. famous London printer (whose mother-in-law was Emma Hamilton's first employer) had appointed Samuel Sims, bookseller of North Parade Circulating Library, Bath, to sell prints of the portrait by Beechey (a three-quarter length copy of the portrait in St Andrew's Hall, Norwich), a mezzotint by Edward Bell, and owned by the Corporation of London (presented by Boydell); the price for an impression was 10s 6d (52½p), proof £1 1s (a guinea). In a matter of weeks, *Memoirs and achievements of the right honorable Horatio Lord Viscount Nelson by a Captain of the British Navy*, published by Barrat and Gibbons of Bath was advertised.

Nelson is remembered in Bath by the bronze plaque on 2 Pierrepont Street, the first house in which he came to stay in 1781. It was unveiled at a parade of cadets in April 1904 by the First Lord of the Admiralty, Lord Selbourne, who gave a rousing speech on the dedication of mariners and the dangers that might befall them as with the then recent loss of the 'A1' submarine. The event closed with three cheers for Lord Selbourne and Mr Bosoni, cornet player from the Pump Room Orchestra, playing 'The Death of Nelson'.

Bath, as reported in the local press, marked the centenary in 1905 with flags flown around the City while on the Technical College hung a framed portrait in laurels of Nelson amongst the flags. A reproduction in the local papers of the *London Gazette* of 1805, and a 'Nelson Sunday' dedicated by the British and Foreign Sailors Society, with various church services were the sum of the centenary.

There are various streets named in memory of Nelson in Bath: Nelson Place, Nelson Place West (started in 1815, left partially completed and derelict for 150

In April 1904 Lord Selbourne, First Lord of the Admiralty, before a parade of cadets, unveiled a plaque on 2 Pierrepont Street to commemorate Nelson's stay there in 1781 and subsequently in 1784 and 1788. His dedication speech recalled the uncertainties and sacrifice of life at sea. Photograph, Bath Library.

years before completion), Nelson Terrace, Nelson Villas, and there is Trafalgar Road in Weston. Nile Street was named three years after the Battle.

Bath Museums contain many artefacts relating to Nelson. In the Guildhall is a portrait of Doctor Woodward, Nelson's first doctor in Bath, by Beach; a white marble bust of Nelson in the style of Thaller and Ransom with a cloak over his shoulder; a plaster cast of the bust by Gahaghan of 1800 (whose family had a workshop in Walcot Street), and a 20th century popularist historical painting of 'Nelson leaving Portsmouth for the last time' by Fred Roe. The collection in the Holburne Museum in Sydney Gardens, started by Francis Holburne a midshipman in the *Orion* at Trafalgar, includes a box made from the companionway steps by which Nelson was taken to the cockpit of the *Victory*, an inscribed Boulton Medal for Trafalgar in white metal, a crystal glass rummer inscribed 'St Vincent 1797', a porcelain coffee can and saucer from the Copenhagen service by A Neale and Co., Caughley 1801, presented by the Reverend Hugh Nelson Ward in 1947, a portrait of Emma Hamilton as a peasant girl by Romney, and a miniature of Captain John Jervis (Earl St Vincent) by Spicer, 1782.

The Bath Library has in its collection three original letters written by Nelson, one written in Bath on his last visit in 1798 to Mr Lloyd, describing the beauty of the women in Bath, and two to a Reverend Beaver, letters of thanks dated 1801, and the original manuscript for Carola Oman's (Lady Lenanton) definitive biography of Nelson written at Flax Bourton near Bristol and published in 1947.

In the Bath Royal Literary and Scientific Institute is a phial with liquid that preserved Nelson's body, as well four oval paintings by Cassali in the ceiling of the first floor room, from William Beckford's Fonthill Abbey (which Nelson and the Hamilton's visited in 1800).

By the end of the 18th century Bath lost its unique position as a Spa with rising medical costs, a preference for private instead of public entertainment, a banking crisis, and competition from Cheltenham and Brighton; the wealth evaporated and it fell into decline. This produced an opportunity for naval officers as a suitable place for retirement and certainly many officers who knew and served with Nelson came to Bath: Captain Berry who had been present at three of Nelson's famous victories, William Hargood who had been a midshipman under Nelson, later to command the *Bellisle* at Trafalgar, to midshipmen who began their naval career, such as Norwich Duff who served with his father in the *Mars* at Trafalgar. (See below the section on Nelson contemporaries.)

Bath and Jane Austen are synonymous, her family came to stay in Queen Square in 1798, but in 1805 she lived several doors down in Sydney Parade from Fanny Nelson. Her brother Francis Austen, Captain to Admiral Louis in *Canopus*, dined on board *Victory* before the Battle of Trafalgar. William, Earl Nelson, married a young widow, Hilare Barlow, after the death of his first wife Sarah, in the hope of producing an heir after the death of his son Horatio in 1806. It was a fruitless union and on the death of the Earl, the Countess moved to Gormersham Park, Kent, the prototype for Jane Austen's Mansfield Park. The Countess was to marry her third and last husband, George Knight, who was Jane Austen's nephew. The other literary connection is that Edmund Nelson encountered a parson named Brunty in Bath, who, in honour of Nelson and his recently acquired Sicilian Estate, changed his name to Bronte, and hence the novelist Bronte sisters, Charlotte, Anne and Emily

After Nelson's death, Emma Hamilton visited Bath on at least two occasions although she had been there before. It is not certain but suggested that she first came as part of the quack Dr Graham's presentation, the 'Temple of Love'. She certainly worked for a famous musical family from Bath, the Linley family, who gave her some musical training when she was employed in London. Later, in 1791, Emma came as the newly married Lady Hamilton and gave a performance of her 'Attitudes' for Lord Charlemont and the Duchess of Devonshire in the Royal Crescent. Sir William Hamilton's first wife, Catherine Barlow, and her mother, a Skrine of Warleigh, Bathford, spent their time between Milford Haven, Bath, and London. Both Emma and Fanny were in Bath at the same time in 1809, Emma in deep mourning driven around the City crying out at the loss of her beloved Nelson.

Horatia, Nelson and Emma's daughter, married the Reverend Philip Ward, and their eldest son, the Reverend Horatio Nelson Ward, became Rector in the coal-mining town of Radstock near Bath, where he and his brother, Marmaduke Ward RN, are buried in the churchyard. The Radstock Museum has a display on Nelson that includes a dress worn by Horatia. Her grandson, the Reverend Hugh Nelson Ward, lived in Marlborough Buildings and later in a nursing home at 7 The Circus. He died in 1952 and donated to the National Maritime Museum, Greenwich, an archive known as the Nelson Ward papers relating to Emma Hamilton and her daughter Horatia.

Since evacuation in the Second World War the Royal Corps of Naval Constructors have operated from Bath, designing vessels and the management of the Fleet of the Royal Navy. Part of this responsibility is HMS *Victory*, still in commission and managed today as a 'minor ship' with the help of the *Victory* Advisory and Technical Committee. Her restoration began in 1950, with 'the great repair ' and will be hopefully complete for the Trafalgar centenary of 2005.

The famous music festival, 'The Bath Festival', took the opportunity to consolidate its finances 'to stimulate a sense of identity and civic pride in Bath to offer the greatest outdoor event the city had ever witnessed' by celebrating the 150th anniversary of the Battle of Trafalgar in 1955, and Nelson's association with the city. A 'Son et Lumiere' involving 600 people, designed at Glynebourne, an hour long was show in three acts. The First Sea Lord and Countess Mountbatten dined with Earl and Countess Nelson as guests of the Mayor, and later attended the show. The Naval and Marine detachment from the Plymouth Division, took part and paraded past 2 Pierrepont Street, with Rear Admiral Sayer (Vice Controller of the Navy) taking the salute before an inspection by Lord Mountbatten outside the Guildhall. It was an ill- starred event from the start with the live broadcast being interrupted and with snow midway through the production cancelling the remaining performances. The losses could not be borne by the Council and the following year the Festival was cancelled.

WHERE THE NELSONS STAYED IN BATH

Reverend Edmund Nelson:
Pierrepont Street, no. 9 (1781)
Milsom Street (1794)
New King Street, nos 10, 17 (1794-97)
Bennett Street, no. 2 (1782-3, 1784, 1797)
Charles Street, no. 22 (1797)
South Parade, no. 3 (1801)
Somerset Street, no. 6
Great Pulteney Street (1802)

Horatio Nelson
Pierrepont Street, no. 2 (1781, 1784, 1788)
New King Street, no. 17 (1797)
Abbey Green, no. 11 (1798)

Frances, Lady Nelson
Pierrepont Street, no. 2 (1788)
New King Street, nos 10, 17 (1794, 1797, 1805)
Bennett Street, no. 2 (1797, 1802, 1809)
Abbey Green, no. 11 (1798)
Kensington Place, no. 2 (1801)
Sydney Parade, no. 14 (1805)
Russell Street, no. 8 (1810, 1815)

Ann Nelson
New King Street (1783)

George and Katherine Matcham (née Nelson)
Kensington Place, no. 19 (1799)
Portland Place, no. 2 (1804, 1805)

Emma, Lady Hamilton
Visit with Sir William Hamilton on honeymoon 1791
Great Pulteney Street, nos 12, 72 (1809)
Edward Street, no. 6 (1814)

NELSON'S CONTEMPORARIES WHO STAYED, LIVED, OR DIED IN BATH

Andrews, Elizabeth (1762-1837). Nelson proposed to her in St Omer in France in 1783 when he had gone to improve his French. In 1786 he took her brother George to sea with him as midshipman in *Boreas*, later in *Agamemnon*, rising to First Lieutenant, Prize Captain of *Ça Ira* in 1795, promoted to Captain, died 1810 Post Captain. Her first marriage was to a clergyman named Farror, her second to Colonel Roger Warne in the East India Service. Lived at 3 St James Square, Bath, with her second husband. Died in Bath.

Ballard (1764-1829). Vice Admiral. Spent most of his naval career in the West Indies, fought at Cape St Vincent in 1780, and under Howe at the Glorious First of June, joined Nelson in 1804, took part in the 'Great Chase' to the West Indies, posted 1806 to Cape Station, 1812 left 'active' list. Lived 34 Park Street, 1825-9.

Barrington, Hon. Samuel (1729-1800). Admiral, 5th son of Irish peer, entered the Navy 1740, Lieutenant 1746, Post Captain 1747 aged 18 years (!) and given command of the *Bellona* (30 guns), captured the first *Raisonnable* in 1757, along whose lines Nelson's first ship was built. Rear Admiral of the White 1778, defeat of D'Estaing off St Lucia 1779, promoted Rear Admiral of the Blue 1782, Admiral of the White 1794, General of the Marines 1799. Friend and fellow captain of Nelson's uncle Maurice Suckling, whose permission he sought to join the Navy. Also an acquaintance of Fanny Nelson. Brother of Daines Barrington (naturalist) who was instrumental in the Arctic Expedition of 1773 in which Nelson served in *Carcass*. Died at 1 Abbey Green.

Bayntun, Henry William, Admiral Sir (1766-1840); Lieutenant 1783, promoted by John Jervis to sloop *Avenger* in 1793, fought at Martinique; most of his service spent in the West Indies. Appointed to the *Leviathan* 1804, commanded at Trafalgar, carried Nelson's guidon in the water procession from Greenwich, 1807. Stationed off Buenos Aires in the Africa 1809, appointed to the *Milford* 1811-12, commanded *Royal Sovereign* yacht, saw no further active service. Rear Admiral 1813, Vice Admiral 1821, Admiral 1837. Lived at 4 St James Square.

Beckford, Sir William (1759-1844); 2nd cousin of Sir William Hamilton, who had entertained Nelson and the Hamiltons in 1800 at Fonthill, Wiltshire, which was sold in 1820 before Beckford moved to Lansdown Crescent, occupying two houses with a classical garden leading up to his tower on the 'downs' that housed his two separate Classical and Gothic libraries at its base (open to the public). Died in Bath and is buried in the graveyard adjoining Beckford's Tower on Lansdown.

Berry, Sir Edward, Bart. (1768-1831). Volunteered 1779, served with Howe at the Glorious First of June 1794, Lieutenant in *Captain* passenger, lead boarding parties at battle of Cape St Vincent, 14 February 1797. Captain of the *Vanguard* at the Battle of the Nile, 1 August 1798, commanded the *Agamemnon* at Trafalgar, 21 October 1805, *Agamemnon* at San Domingo 1806, commanded *Royal Sovereign* yacht 1813-14, Rear Admiral 1821. Lived the last three years of his life in Bath at 2 Gay Street, where he died in 1831. Buried with full Naval honours, the service conducted by Archdeacon Mosey, DD, the pall was supported by Admirals Bayntun, J. Bullen, Cunningham, R. Dacres and Fitzgerald, walking Captains Browne, Buckle, Carden, Carrl, Clay, Connolly, Garretts, Gordon, Jervoise, Jones, Lye, Mainwaring, Garwen Roberts, Saunders, Sykes, Tobin, Vasobra, Vincent, and many more

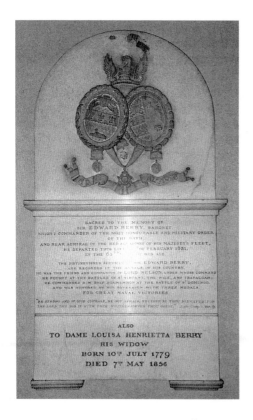

Admiral Sir Edward Berry's plaque in St Swithin's Church, Walcot. His damaged gravestone can be seen in the adjoining graveyard propped against the wall. Berry and his wife Louisa, who had lived at 2 Gay Street, were great friends of the Nelsons. At Berry's funeral with full Naval Honours in 1831 Admirals: Bayntun, Bullen, Cunning-ham, Dacres and Fitzgerald, supported the pall.

unidentified Naval officers. Too frail to attend the service, Admiral Bickerton, as the senior officer, attended in his coach. At St Swithin's Church, London Street, Walcot, there is a memorial tablet in white marble (on the left as you enter the church). A disintegrating tombstone in adjoining churchyard, from Berry's tomb, includes the name of his widow Louisa Henrietta Berry (1779-1856), companion to Lady Nelson when she lived at Roundwood near Ipswich.

Bickerton, Richard Hussey, Admiral (1760-1832). Son of Admiral Sir Richard Bickerton, Bart (1725-92) who made his name in the West Indies, Nelson met him while in Bath in 1781. Entered the Navy 1774, Lieutenant 1777, first posting under Charles Middleton (Lord Barham). A contemporary of Nelson's in the West Indies, married Ann Athill, a belle of English Harbour in Nevis 1778, a good friend of Mrs Nelson in Bath. Prior to Mediterranean service blockaded Cadiz 1799 and was part of Abercrombie's invasion of Egypt in 1801. Had served with Nelson as second-in-command in the Mediterranean in 1803 for two years. At the time of Trafalgar, Admiral of the Red, from whom Nelson sought intelligence as Bickerton returned home on sick leave as they passed the Scillies, as the *Victory* sped to the Mediterranean. Lived at 15 The Circus, died in Bath. Plaque by Sir Francis Chantrey in the south aisle, Bath Abbey.

Bridport, Alexander Hood, Viscount (1726-1814), younger brother of Samuel Lord Hood, entered the Navy in 1741, served during the Seven Years War under Hawke in the Channel and the Mediterranean 1793, second-in-command under Howe at the Glorious First of June, knighted after partial defeat of French 1790 whilst in command of *Victory* 1797, in command of the Fleet at Spithead when the crews mutinied, made Commander-in-Chief, Channel Fleet on the death of Lord Howe in 1799. Retired 1800, created Viscount 1801. Died at 34 Great Pulteney Street,

Browne, Thomas, Rear Admiral (1787-1849). He confirmed that Foley had no charts at the Battle of the Nile, 1798, and that just observation determined Foley's course in sailing inside the French fleet, between them and the shore. In *Foudroyant* at the trial of Carricciolo, 1800, First Lieutenant in *Elephant* under Captain Foley, Nelson's flagship at the Battle of Copenhagen in 1801, entered July 1800, discharged 6 April 1801. Lived at 5 Green Park Buildings and 16 Catherine Place.

Bullen, Joseph, Admiral (1760-1845). Entered the Navy in 1774 under Captain W. Cornwallis. Lieutenant 1778 served under Nelson in the *Hitchinbrooke*, went up the San Juan River, Nicaragua, 1793 served with Nelson in the *Agamemnon*, his first command prize was *Muette*, involved in the siege in Corsica of the town of Bastia, invalided home after being burnt by red hot shot, resumed briefly his career at sea, in 1796, promoted to Post Captain, commanded Sea Fencibles on the East Coast. Had 28 years active service. Married Margaret Ann Seafe in 1801, buried in Bathwick Churchyard. Lived at 13 Raby Place.

Clarence, William, Duke of, later King William IV (1765-1837). First introduced off New York by Lord Hood in 1782, Nelson's aide-de-camp in the West Indies in 1786, best man at Nelson's wedding in Nevis in 1787, rose to the rank of Rear Admiral. He was a lifelong correspondent with Nelson once he had left the Navy, later became Lord High Admiral under George IV, and eventually became King William IV. Stayed at 103 Sydney Gardens, made an Honorary Freeman of the City of Bath in 1817.

Connolly, Matthew, Captain (1776-1853). Born Chatham, entered the Navy 1787, captured by the French under Captain William Hargood in *Hyaena* in 1793, commanded one of the launches that took part in the bombardment of Cadiz under Nelson in 1797, lost three men, spent 14 years as a Lieutenant before promotion. Published report on gunnery and 'divisions' adopted in ships by the Navy. Lived at 8 and 25 Stanhope Street. Plaque in south aisle (close to Hargood and Duff), Bath Abbey.

Cosby, Philip, Admiral of the Red (1730-1808). Entered the Navy 1743, under the patronage of Captain Spry, saw service in both the West and East Indies, his zeal came to the attention of General Wolfe who chose him as his marine aide-de-camp at Quebec 1754, distinguished himself off Long Island in command of the *Robust*, Receiver General St Kitts 1771, flew pennant in the *St George* as Port Admiral Plymouth before, third in command in the Mediterranean in 1793 in the *Windsor Castle* under Lord Hood whilst Nelson served in the *Agamemnon*, present at the capture of Toulon and Corsica. Frances Nelson met him in Bath 1794. Lived at 4 Alfred Street. Plaque in south aisle in Bath Abbey.

Day, Captain. Nelson recommends to Admiral Jervis the attributes of the then Lieutenant Day for his ' indefatigable, attention and ability' as Agent of Transports, 'this zealous officer' with his services in evacuating Corsica in 1796. Lived at 14 Church Street, Bathwick.

Drake, John, Vice Admiral (1788-1864). Entered the Navy June 1804 as 1st Class Volunteer Midshipman in *Defiance* under Captains Dundas and Hotham in Admiral

Calder's action before Trafalgar, present at Trafalgar, Midshipman/Master's Mate until 1810, saw various actions off the French coast. Followed Admiral Hotham into the *Northumberland* as First Lieutenant. Senior Lieutenant of *Albion* at Navarino, 1827. Died in Bath.

Duff, Norwich, Vice Admiral (1792-1862). Served as midshipman in his father's ship *Mars* at Trafalgar in which both his brother and father were killed, entered the *Euryalus* and later *Ajax* under Admiral Blackwood who undertook the pupillage of the young midshipman after the loss of his father, saw service in the Dardanelles, made First Lieutenant at the Battle of Lissa (March 1811 in the Adriatic), on active service until 1820. Married Helen Scholbred of Bath and had five children, lived 10 Marlborough Buildings. Died in Bath, brass memorial plaque in the south aisle of Bath Abbey above Hargood.

Duncan, Adam, Viscount, Admiral (1731-1804). Defeated the Dutch fleet at the Battle of Camperdown in October 1797, although Nelson never met him, genuinely celebrated his victory, but Nelson was wary that it might eclipse the victory at Cape St Vincent in February 1797. Nelson wrote a letter of condolence to Duncan's second son, Henry, a Lieutenant in the *Royal Sovereign* and made offer of a command in 1804. Made a Freeman of the City of Bath. Lived at 44 Great Pulteney Street, 1796-1801.

Gambier, James, Admiral Lord (1723-89). Member of the Navy Board, second-in-command in New York to Howe on the America Station. During the Seven Years War with France, returned home having captured 64 prizes amounting to 2000 guns, Commander-in-Chief North America Station 1778-80, also Jamaica Station 1783-4 whilst Nelson was in the *Boreas* in the West Indies. Died at 12 Brock Street, Bath.

Gardner, Alan, Admiral Lord (1742-1808). Major General of the Marines. Contemporary of Admiral Barrington, present at the capture of the French vessel *Raisonnable* whose design was used for the first ship Nelson entered in the Royal Navy. Temporarily Commander-in-Chief Jamaica Station 1785 when Nelson was in the Leeward Islands, a good friend of Nelson. Appointed Lord High Admiral 1790, distinguished himself in command of *The Queen* at the Glorious First of June in 1794 under Howe. One of the admirals who negotiated at the Mutiny at Spithead in 1797, sent with fleet of 16 ships to join Nelson in the Mediterranean 1799, commander of fleet off Ireland 1800 that intercepted the French invasion. Dined with Nelson and his agent Alexander Davison in Portsmouth when he was

Commander-in-Chief Portsmouth and where Nelson was about to join *Victory* in 1803. Died aboard his ship in the Channel. Memorial plaque in the south transept, Bath Abbey.

Gordon, Captain (died 1842?). Served in *Polyphemus* as Lieutenant in October 1805 as part of Nelson's fleet, recommends for promotion to William Marsden, Secretary to the Admiralty. Lived at 1 Nelson Place.

Hargood, Sir William, Admiral (1760-1839). Son of a purser, Hezekiah Hargood, served under Nelson as a midshipman in the *Bristol* in 1777, patron Admiral Hyde Parker, 1780 served under the Duke of Clarence as a Lieutenant and attended Nelson's wedding, Captain of *Magnificent* at the Battle of the Saintes 1782, under Rodney, commanded *Belleisle* at Trafalgar in 1805 having returned from a cruise in the East Indies that included China, completed 40 years in the Royal Navy as Superintendent at Plymouth Dockyard. His wife published a volume on his exploits. Lived at 25 Queen Square and died at 9 Royal Crescent. Buried in Bath Abbey, the pall bearers at his funeral Admirals Bayntun, Hotham, Fitzgerald, Sykes, Bullen, O'Bryen.

Holburne, Sir Francis, Baron of Menstrie (1793-1874). Descended from a distinguished naval family, grandfather Sir Francis Holburne, Admiral of the White, Rear Admiral of Great Britain, Governor of Greenwich and MP for Plymouth. Entered the navy as 1st Class Volunteer in *Orion* under Captain Codrington (Family Seat, Dodington House near Bath) at Trafalgar, midshipman 1808, assisted with the landings at Corunna, Lieutenant 1813, first command *Stromboli*, served in *Foudroyant* in Brazil 1813, present at the sinking of Nelson's ship *Agamemnon* in the River Plate, Uruguay. Ended active service in the Channel Fleet. Founder of the Holburne and Menstrie Museum, Sydney Garden, Bath. Lived and died at 10 Cavendish Crescent, Bath, buried Lansdown Cemetery.

Hood, Samuel, Admiral, Viscount (1724-1816). Entered the Navy in 1740, Lieutenant 1746, 1754 Commander, 1756 Post Captain, served under Boscawen, Rodney, 1778 Commissioner of Portsmouth Dockyard, 1780 Admiral of the Blue, 1781 defeated DeGrasse off Martinique, 1782 battle for Frigate Bay, Nelson's commander in the West Indies where he introduced Nelson to the Duke of Clarence in 1783, Nelson considered himself 'as treated like a son', 1788 Commissioner to the Navy, Commander-in-Chief Mediterranean 1793-5 to Nelson, commanded as Brigadier General at the siege of Toulon 1793, in command at the siege of Bastia where Nelson lost the sight in his eye, visited Frances Nelson whilst in Bath, staying at 16 Milsom Street 1795, Governor of Greenwich Hospital, Elder of Trinity House, a chief mourner at Nelson's funeral at St Paul's Cathedral in 1806, also recorded as staying in 5 Queen Square, 1806-7. Died in Bath.

Hood, Sir Alexander, 2nd Baron Bridport (1788-1864). Married Nelson's niece Charlotte Nelson, Duchess of Bronte, daughter of William 1st Earl Nelson. Charlotte went to school in Bath and met Lady Nelson with her parents in Bath in 1811. Charlotte inherited the Bronte Estate and it remained in the family until the 1980s. Bridport was executor to Lady Nelson's will and codicils, the last being written on the day before she died in May 1831. Buried in the Chapel at the family home of Cricket St Thomas in Somerset. Lived at 94 New Sydney Place.

Hotham, Admiral Sir William (1736-1814). Nephew of Admiral Sir William Hotham (1788-1864). Entered the Navy in 1786, sailed to Guinea under Admiral Thompson, 1794, Lieutenant in *Victory* under Lord Hood commanding the Mediterranean Fleet, served under Nelson ashore in Corsica at the siege of Bastia, 1797, Channel Fleet in command of *Adamant* at the Battle of Camperdown, 1803, blockaded Boulogne, 1804, left active service, briefly in command of the Liverpool Fencibles. On promotion to Flag rank in 1813 given command of the yacht *Royal Sovereign*. A gentleman-in-waiting to the King, wrote a gossipy volume called *Characters principally Professional*, and disapproved of Nelson's public humiliation of 'Fanny'. Often visited 'Fanny' when in Bath after Trafalgar, up to her death in 1831. Lived at 10 Cavendish Place in 1819, and 2 Widcombe Crescent. Died Windsor, buried near Reading.

Howe, Admiral Earl Richard (1726-99). Left Eton 1740 to go to sea, sailed with Commodore Anson, served under Boscawen and Hawke, Lord of, and later Treasurer to the Admiralty, MP for Dartmouth, 1782 created a Viscount, relieved the siege of Gibraltar, First Lord of the Admiralty 1783 to 1788. Summoned from Bath to rejoin Fleet, victor at the Glorious First of June, 1794. Nelson petitioned Howe in 1793 for a command whilst 'on the beach', met after the loss of arm in 1797 at audience with the King. Retired from active service due to ill health to Bath for the cure in 1797. Earl St Vincent describes in a letter to Nelson that Howe is summoned from Bath by the King to be created the first Knight of the Garter in the Royal Navy. Stayed at 71 Great Pulteney Street.

Laugharne, William (1758-1856). Entered the Navy as a young gentleman in *Foudroyant*, 80 guns, with Nelson witnessed the surrender of Naples 1799, present at the capture of the *Genereux* and the *Ville de Marseille* (that escaped after the Battle of the Nile) 1800, followed Captain Berry into the *Princess Charlotte* and *Ruby* saw service in the Mediterranean, North Sea, and Baltic. Lieutenant 1806, finished the Napoleonic War as Flag Lieutenant Malta under the command of his uncle. Died in Bath aged 71 years.

LeBrun, Virgée (1755, 1842). Swiss artist, first major commission for Marie Antoinette in 1798, admitted to the French Academy, escaped to Italy after the French Revolution where she met the Hamiltons. Painted a miniature of Emma as a 'Bacchante' for Sir William Hamilton. On his death in 1803 he left an enamel version by Henry Bone, RA, to Nelson in his will as a testament 'to his friendship' (now in The Wallace Collection, Manchester Square, London). Lived at 34 Gay Street.

Lely, Peter. Captain of the Marines in *Revenge*, 74 guns, at Trafalgar. Died in Bath 1832.

Mainwaring, Thomas Francis, Rear Admiral (1780-1858). Entered the Royal Navy Academy 1793, 1796 Volunteer, 1800 Lieutenant in *Naiad*, 38 guns, under Captain Dundas repeater ship (signals) at Trafalgar, 1806 Commander, subsequently in the Baltic 1810 to the end of hostilities, in command of the *Royal George*. Lived Westmorland Place, and at 29 Marlborough Buildings. Buried Walcot burial ground.

Palmer, Edmund, Captain, CB (1782-1834). Son of John Palmer who owned and ran the Theatre Royal of Bath and Bristol, first Post Master General, Mayor and MP for Bath. In correspondence with Nelson over the promotion of his son, Nelson wrote to his father congratulating the promotion to commodore of his son. Palmer whilst in command of the *Hebrus.* in March 1814 engaged the French frigate *L'Etoile*; after a protracted engagement, the French ship struck her colours, the last to do so in the Napoleonic wars. The tricolour was presented to Earl St Vincent whose great niece he married in 1817. Memorial plaque by West Door, Bath Abbey.

Phillip, Arthur, Admiral (1738 -1814). Joined the Navy as a midshipman, 1775 served two years with the Portuguese Navy. 1787 commanded the first convoy to Australia establishing Sydney and the first penal colony. Known socially to the Nelsons, 1797 whilst in command of *Swiftsure*, despite unrest amongst the crew, Nelson inspected the ship and reported to St Vincent that it was in 'excellent order and fit for any service'. Phillip's last command of *Blenheim* in 1798 superseded by Admiral Frederick, and he was not re-appointed to the *Swiftsure*, thus missing the

Battle of the Nile. Nelson wrote to his wife in 1798, 'Governor Phillip is a good man remember me kindly to him there'. 1803 Inspector of Sea Fencibles. Lived at 19 Bennett Street, 1810-14. Died in Bath, buried at Bathford Church.

Pocock, Nicholas (1740-1821). Bristol-born, master mariner turned painter to the Admiralty, Lord Hood, when Commissioner to the Navy, a patron. Painted Nelson's battles as illustrations for the first serious biography, *The Life and Services of Horatio, Viscount Nelson, from his Lordships Mesrs, James Clarke and John McArthur*, 1809, contributor to *The Naval Chronicle*. Lived at 36 St James's Parade in 1817.

Popham, Home, Rear Admiral (1762-1820). Entered the Navy in 1778, survey in Africa, 1781, made Lieutenant, 1787 went on a private business trip to the East Indies, 1793 re-enlisted as Agent for Transport to Duke of York's Army in Holland, Post Captain 1795, employed on Sea Fencibles 1798, Fellow of the Royal Society 1799, created Knight of the Order of St John by the Tsar of Russia, 1800-3 Red Sea to assist Wellesley, 1804 worked with Robert Fulton on new weapons. Captured Cape Town 1806, Denmark Captain of the Fleet under Gambier, 1810-12 Corunna landing troops, 1815 design for semaphore stations. The 'Marine Vocabulary' devised at his own expense were the signal flags used at Trafalgar for Nelson's signal, 'England Expects That Every Man Will Do His Duty'. The breakthrough in signalling was the ability of communicating phrases with individual flags as well as being able to spell words with only 33 flags, first version developed in 1803. Lived at 9 Portland Place, Bath, 1820.

Robertson, William, Rear Admiral. Entered 1803 as midshipman in *Defence*, 74 guns, served in the North Sea and at Trafalgar, moved to *Fame* 1807 as Master's Mate, taken prisoner at Copenhagen but escaped. 1809 entered in *Victory* under Sir James Saumarez, 1810 Lieutenant. Served in the West Indies 1811, 1814-15 second-in-command to John Ross in his expedition to find the North West Passage. 1820 South America Station Furst Lieutenant in *Diamond*, Flag Lieutenant to Captain Hardy in Lisbon, made Commander 1827, active service until 1837. Married Elizabeth Pater of Bristol. Lived at 11 Widcombe Crescent. Died in Bath.

Robinson, Mark, Rear Admiral (1722-99). Entered Navy at 14 years, fought under Warren and Hawke, distinguished role at the reduction of Guadeloupe, 1771, presented with 'plate' for saving the town of Charleston. Robertson served under Nelson as acting lieutenant in *Worcester* in 1776, invalided home in 1781 after the loss of his leg in action under Admiral Graves at Chesapeake. Known in the city for his wooden leg. Lived at 20 Henrietta Street. Died at Bath.

Robinson, Thomas Pitt (died 1861). Only son of the above, entered the Navy in 1804 as volunteer 1st class in *Swiftsure* commanded by his father, serving in the Mediterranean under Nelson. Transferred in May 1805 as midshipman in *Royal Sovereign* at Trafalgar, 1806-11 served off Cadiz in *Ocean* and *Queen*, 1812 Lieutenant, 1813-15 in *Tigris* Irish Station, paid off 1818. Re-commissioned 1827, 1828 ranked Commander due to service of grandfather and father in the Navy, ended career in the service of the Coastguard 1837-40. Lived 20 Henrietta Street and died in Bath.

Rodney, Sir George, Admiral (1750-1820). Both Nelson and Rodney were in the Caribbean at the same time, Nelson in Nicaragua, Rodney sought the French, culminating in the Battle of the Saintes in 1787, where he defied tradition and 'broke the line' to victory. Stayed in 1764 and 1783 at 14 Gay Street, Bath.

St Vincent, Sir John Jervis, Earl (1735-1823). Entered the Navy 1749 as midshipman, distinguished himself in the Seven Years War and the War of American Independence, rising to Vice-Admiral in 1793, commanded fleet in *Victory* at the Battle of Cape St Vincent, 14 February 1797, in which Commodore Nelson of *Captain*, 74 guns, distinguished himself, subsequently Commander-in-Chief the Mediterranean in 1798 at the time of the Battle of the Nile, also of Channel Fleet when Nelson was in command of coastal defences along the Channel 1801, later First Lord of the Admiralty, appointed Nelson to command the Mediterranean Fleet 1803, leading to victory at the Battle of Trafalgar in 1805. Visited his sister, Mrs Ricketts, at 8 Argyle Street in 1783, 1797, 1801 and 1816. Made a Freeman of the City of Bath in 1797.

Shirley, Thomas, General (died 1800). Captain General of the Leeward Islands, complained of Nelson's enforcement of the 'Navigation Acts' in 1784, writing 'high ranking officers ... are jealous of being dictated to in their duty by very young gentlemen'. In reply, Nelson wrote, 'he had the honour of being as old as the Prime Minister and as capable of commanding His Majesty's Ship as the Prime Minister governs Great Britain.' Despite their differences Nelson dined with the General in 1786 and an acquaintance of Frances Nelson in Bath. Lived at 35 Gay Street. Buried in Bath Abbey, plaque in north aisle.

Slade, Sir Thomas (1703-1771). Surveyor to the Navy 1755 to 1771. According to the *Bath Chronicle* arrived in the company of a Lady, 14 February, died 21 February. Highly respected Surveyor to the Navy, whose influence in ship design was still relevant ten years after his death. Instrumental in developing the work horse of the

Georgian navy the 74-gun ship. Remembered for the design and overseeing the building of the *Victory* at Chatham Dockyard, launched in 1765, flagship at the Battle of Cape St Vincent, 14 February 1797, and Nelson's flagship at the Battle of Trafalgar, 21 October 1805.

Smith, Sir William Sydney, Vice Admiral (1746-1840). Knight Grand Cross of the Tower and Sword, Companion of the Imperial Ottoman Order of the Crescent, Hero of the Siege at Acre, at which British and Turkish troops halted Napoleon's army of the Orient, and organised a truce by which the French troops would be repatriated in 1799. A charismatic commander who Nelson mistrusted after he failed to burn the entire French fleet after the British occupation of Toulon in 1793, and who also resented that Smith had his own squadron when Nelson was the senior officer in the Mediterranean in 1798, although when pushed had a grudging respect for him. Smith was to join Nelson's fleet in 1805, armed with rockets and projectiles to harass the enemy, but was thwarted by the Battle of Trafalgar. His parents had met in Bath, he attended Bath Grammar School, 1772-4. Visited his mother, Mary Thurlow, in 1798 welcomed by the whole City. Lived at 12 Catherine Place. Died in Paris, buried there in Père Lachaise cemetery.

Southey, Robert (1774-1843). Poet Laureate. Born in Bristol, attended the Grammar School in Bath. Commissioned to write a biography of Nelson which appeared in 1813, overwhelmed by the task and assisted by his brother, Thomas, Lieutenant in *Bellona* at the Battle of Copenhagen, 1801, in the detail. Produced the most widely read biography which has run to over a hundred editions, and never been out of print. Lived at Westgate Buildings and with his aunt at 108 Walcot Street.

Sykes, John, Vice Admiral. Entered the Navy 1783 as Captain's servant in *Resource*, 1789 midshipman *Princess Charlotte* yacht, 1790 Master's mate in *Discovery* under Vancouver. Lieutenant 1795, followed Admiral Vandeput in various vessels until 1798. Commander 1800. First command, bomb vessel *Hecla* 1803, transferred to *Nautilus* 1805. Nelson writes to him whilst in command of the sloop *Nautilus* September 1805 to cruise off Cape St Vincent to intercept ships sent in reinforcement of Nelson's fleet and inform them as to his position. After Trafalgar Sykes encountered Lieutenant La Penotiére in the schooner *Pickle* sailing with the official Trafalgar dispatches from Collingwood; Sykes sails for Plymouth and onto London. Both La Penotiere and Sykes arrive within ten minutes of each other at the Admiralty Gates in Whitehall at 1.30am, 6 November 1805, to inform Lord Barham, First Lord of the Admiralty, of the news of the Great Victory and the sad loss of Lord Nelson. 1806 Post Captain, on active service until 1836. Lived 19 Royal Crescent.

Wolfe, James, General (1727- 1759), of Quebec. Nelson's hero, after hearing of his exploits as a boy helped by the prints of his dramatic death after a painting by Benjamin West, at the 'Heights of Abraham'. Visited with his parents Lord Inchiquoin, stayed at 5 Trim Street in 1754. On a return visit to Bath, he was clandestinely engaged to a wealthy heiress, a Miss Lowther ten years his junior. Whilst in the City he was entertained by Earl of Chatham, William Pitt (MP for Bath 1755-63) at 7 The Circus in 1759 where he received orders to embark for Canada. It was John Jervis, later Earl St Vincent, who was Wolfe's ship's captain and messenger to Miss Lowther of her fiancee's death. In 1793 Nelson speculated on how Wolfe would have tackled the Siege of Bastia in Bastia.

Wolsely, William, Captain. Master of *Lowestoffe* December 1792 to March 1794 (the same ship in which Nelson served as Second Lieutenant under Captain William Locker, his 'Sea Daddy' in 1771), later the *Imperieuse*, 38 guns, seized from the French at the occupation of Toulon in 1793, gunnery commended by Nelson after the Siege of Bastia in 1794. March 1801 to April 1802 commanded *San Josef*, 100 guns, a Spanish prize from the Battle of Cape St Vincent captured by Nelson in 1797. The Admiral had been on board briefly in February 1801 before joining the *St George* and sailing for Copenhagen. Wolsley died Admiral of the Red. He lived at Catherine Place.

MEMBERS OF NELSON'S CREW FROM BATH

Dillon, Charles. By trade a painter, drowned whilst in *Theseus* November 1796.

Wilton, Richard. Ordinary Seaman in *Elephant* at Copenhagen, 2 April 1801. Entered July 1800.

CHRONOLOGY OF NELSON'S LIFE

1758 Born Burnham Thorpe, Norfolk, 29 September 1758, fourth child of eight surviving of original eleven. Four brothers: Maurice, William, Edmund and Suckling, and three sisters: Susannah, Ann, Catherine. Father, Edmund, rural parson; mother Catherine nèe Suckling

1767 Catherine, Nelson's mother dies.

1770 Nelson persuades his elder brother to write to their father Edmund in Bath for permission to join his uncle, Captain Maurice Suckling of the Royal Navy, who is preparing his ship for war with the Spanish. Entered into the book of the *Raisonnable* as a midshipman.

1771 Joins the *Raisonnable* in the Medway. March transfers to the *Triumph* and sails to the West Indies in a merchant ship.

1772-3 Returns from the West Indies, signs up for expedition to the Arctic in the bomb vessel *Carcass* to find a route to the Pacific, appointed midshipman to the *Seahorse* to the East Indies.

1775-6 Invalided from ship with malaria and returns home.

1777 Passes exam for Lieutenant, Tower Hill, London, appointed to *Lowestoffe*, arrives July at Port Royal, Jamaica.

1778 Uncle Maurice Suckling dies, appointed First Lieutenant in the *Bristol*, given first command, brig *Badger*.

1779 Promoted Post Captain in command of the frigate *Hitchinbrooke*. Spain allies with France against Britain.

1780 Disastrous campaign to Nicaragua. Appointed to the frigate *Janus*. Returns to Britain too ill to take command. Takes the cure in Bath.

1781 Appointed to command frigate *Albermarle* and escorts convoy to the Baltic.

1782 Sails to Quebec, joins Lord Hood's squadron off New York and returns to the West Indies. Almost abandons career for Miss Mary Simpson in Quebec.

1783 Fails to take the Turk Island. June, returns to England. October with peace with France Nelson goes to St Omer to learn French and falls for Miss Elizabeth Andrews.

1784 Returns from France and is appointed to command of the frigate *Boreas*, sails for the West Indies. Arrives English Harbour, Antigua July and meets Mrs Moutray.

1785 Mrs Moutray and family sail for England and Bath in March, in May Nelson meets Mrs Frances Nisbet, widow, on Island of Nevis.

1786 November to March aide-de-camp to Prince William Henry (later Duke of Clarence, subsequently King William IV).

1787 Marries Frances Nisbet at Nevis, Prince William best man at wedding. Returns to England, paid off, and is on half pay.

1788 Visits Bath with his wife. Unemployed in Norfolk.

1793 Re-employed by the Admiralty. Appointed to command of the *Agamemnon*, sails for the Mediterranean. July, off Toulon, September meets the Hamiltons for the first time, October engages French frigates.

1794 Involved with the campaign to secure Corsica as a base for the Mediterranean fleet, injures his right eye at Calvi.

1795 Captures the *Ça Ira* off Toulon, Jervis succeeds Hood as Commander-in-Chief, Mediterranean.

1796 Appointed Commodore, joins the *Captain*.

1797 Leaves the Mediterranean in March. Plays a decisive role in the Battle of Cape St Vincent against the Spanish. Promoted Rear Admiral, created a Knight of the Bath. Hoists flag in the *Theseus*, returns home. July involved in boat actions off Cadiz and abortive attack on Santa Cruz off Tenerife where he loses his right arm. Returns home to Bath.

1798 Hoists flag in March in the *Vanguard*, joins fleet off Cadiz under Earl St Vincent. July, dispatched to pursue the French fleet in the Mediterranean. 1st

August destroys the French fleet at Aboukir Bay, Egypt. Created Baron of the Nile in November. December rescues the Bourbons of Naples, evacuating them to Sicily.

1799 Lord Keith succeeds Earl St Vincent, Nelson remains in the Mediterranean. Created the Duke of Bronte and given Sicilian estate. Transfers flag to the *Foudroyant*. Nelson embroiled with the Hamiltons.

1800 Captures the *Genereux* that had escaped at the Battle of the Nile. Returns home through Europe with the Hamiltons leaving in July. Meets Lady Nelson for last time in London. Spends Christmas with Hamiltons at Fonthill.

1801 Promoted Vice Admiral in January, hoists flag in the *San Josef* he captured at the Battle of Cape St Vincent. Sails for the Baltic and in April defeats the Danish at Copenhagen in *Elephant*. July takes command of the Squadron of Particular Service. Failed attack on Boulogne. Buys Merton Place, Wimbledon, takes seat in the House of Lords.

1802 His father, Reverend Edmund Nelson, dies in Pulteney Street, Bath.

1803 Sir William Hamilton dies. War declared with France. Hoists flag in *Victory*.

1804 Blockades the French Mediterranean ports. Spain declares war on Britain.

1805 French elude the blockade and escape across the Atlantic to the Caribbean, Nelson gives chase. August returns home. September rejoins *Victory*. 21st October the Battle of Trafalgar, Nelson destroys the combined fleet of French and Spanish, mortally wounded.

1806 Buried St Paul's Cathedral, London.

SOURCES AND REFERENCES

Barbeau, A. 'Bath in the Eighteenth Century', *Life and Letters at Bath in the 18th Century*. Bath, 904.

Bath Chronicle.

Bath Journal.

Borsay, P. Oxford. *The Image of Georgian Bath, 1700-2000: Town, Heritage and History*. Bath, 2000.

Cotterell, 'Historic Map of Bath'

Dictionary of National Biography

Drinkwater, Bethune. *A Narrative of the Battle of St Vincent 1797*. London, 1969.

Guerin, Winifred. *Horatia Nelson*. Oxford, 1981.

Green, M. A. *Eighteenth Century Architecture in Bath*. Bath, 1904.

Hibbert, C. *Nelson. A Personal History*. London, 1994.

Hills, A.M. 'Health in the Royal Navy during the age of Nelson', *Royal Naval Medical Service Journal*, Vol 86. 2. 2000, pp. 72-81.

Keate, E. M. *Nelson's Wife*. London, 1939.

Lesley, Flash. 'Known at this Address'. Bath City Council. 1982.

Little Bryan. 'Bath Portrait'. Burleigh Press, 1961.

Mariner's Mirror. Journal of the Society for Nautical Research.

Naval Chronicle 1799-1806, Repr. London, 1998.

The Nelson Dispatch. Magazine of The Nelson Society.

Nicolas, Sir N. H. *Dispatches and Letters of Lord Nelson*. London, 1844; repr. 1997.

Naish, G. P. B. *Nelson's letters to his wife and other documents*. Navy Record Society, London, 1957.

Pocock, Tom. *The Young Nelson in the Americas*. London, 1980.

— *Life of Horatio Nelson*. London, 1987.

— *Nelson's Women*. London, 1999.

Pugh, P. D. Gordon. *Nelson and His Surgeons*. Edinburgh and London, 1968.

O'Byrne, W. R. *Naval Biographical Dictionary*. London, 1849; repr. 2001.

Oman, Carola. *Life of Nelson*. London, 1947, 1974.

Rawson, Geoffrey. *Nelson's Letters* (selected and edited by). London, 1960.

Royal Naval Medical Service Journal. Vol 86. 2. 2000. Dr A. M. Hills, pp. 72-81.

Tyte. *Mineral Waters and Baths in Bath*.

Walker, Richard. *Nelson Portraits*. Portsmouth, 1998.

White, Colin. *1797 Nelson's Year of Destiny*. Stroud, 1998.

Other sources and credits
Victoria Art Gallery, Bath
The Bath Reference Library.
Donald Percy of the Mayoral guides of Bath
K. C. S. Thompson (Spry family)

Back cover: Copy of an engraving of the monument to Nelson in the Great Hall of the Guildhall, City of London, used by Mr King, monumental mason of Bath, to advertise his business.

THE NELSON SOCIETY

The Nelson Society has a world-wide membership and is a registered charity (no. 296979). It was formed at the Norfolk Club in Norwish which, in 1852, had amalgamated with a Nelson Club founded in 1806.

Among its members are many descendants of Nelson and of those who fought with him. Corporate members include towns, libraries, museums and many other associated and interested organisations.

The aims of the Nelson Society are to promote interest in, and appreciation of, the outstanding qualities of leadership and patriotism shown by Lord Nelson. It encourages research into all aspects of his life and times whilst providing a basis for educational work, including studies of British naval developments from the past to the present day. It also brings together many fellow enthusiasts.

The Nelson Society has no headquarters to maintain nor the expense of salaried staff. Regular committee meetings are held and all members receive a free copy of the quarterly journal *The Nelson Dispatch*. This contains articles and news relating to Nelson and his period and members are encouraged to contribute to its lively correspondence column, notes and queries.

The Society's AGM and Annual Dinner are held on the Saturday nearest to Trafalgar Day (21st October) in various places associated with Nelson. Many other visits, talks and social gatherings are held throughout the year. Where possible the Society has provided or helped restore appropriate memorials.

Many other Society publications are available as well as memorabilia and items of interest relating to Nelson and his times.

For details on how to join the Society contact:
The Membership Secretary
The Nelson Society
68 Stamshaw Road
Portsmouth
Hampshire PO2 8LS